BROKEN BELIEVER: NO MORE

ISBN 978-0-9862890-0-2
    978-0-9862890-1-9 (Electronic version)
Editing by: Exclamation Publishing
Cover by: Clarity Consulting & Design
Printed in the United States of America

DEDICATION

I am thankful to God for His grace, mercy, love, and forgiveness.

To all women: Avoid focusing on past failures, instead make the necessary adjustments to step into the future God eloquently planned for you.

To my sons, David and Ovell, thank you for being supportive and loving me. Thank you for the comforting conversations and text messages. I love you very much!

"For I know the plans I have for you," declares the LORD, "plans to prosper you and not to harm you, plans to give you hope and a future."
Jeremiah 29:11 NIV

The Lord will fulfill his purpose for me; your steadfast love, O Lord, endures forever. Do not forsake the work of your hands.
Psalm 138:8 ESV

I thank Christ Jesus our Lord, who has given me strength, that he considered me trustworthy, appointing me to his service.
1 Timothy 1:12

Table of Contents

Introduction

*"Enlarge the place of your tent; stretch your tent curtains wide,
do not hold back; lengthen your cords, strengthen your stakes.
For you will spread out to the right and to the left;
Your descendants will dispossess nations and
settle in their desolate cities.
Do not be afraid; you will not be put to shame.
Do not fear disgrace; you will not be humiliated.
You will forget the shame of your youth and remember
no more the reproach of your widowhood.
For your Maker is your husband—
The Lord Almighty is His name—
He is called the God of all the earth.
The Lord will call you back as if you were a wife
deserted and distressed in spirit—
A wife who married young, only to be rejected, says your God.
For a brief moment I abandoned you, but with deep compassion I
will bring you back. In a surge of anger, I hid my face from you for a
moment,
but with everlasting kindness I will
have compassion on you," says the Lord your Redeemer.*

– Isaiah 54:2-8 NIV

Another morning had come, and I sat in my car staring at the whitewashed hospital plastered against a desert landscape. The city's future nurses were inside waiting for me to come and instruct them through another day of clinical. Here it was another moment in my life, and I was wrestling with constant, nagging feelings of emptiness and uselessness. But my spirit could not take another minute of the wondering—wondering if I was fulfilling God's purpose in my life and wondering if there was more God had in store for me. I was done with another day of wondering.

Because I had arrived to work early, I chose to use the extra time to pray. As I concluded my prayers, my eyes landed on my Bible—never leave home without it. However, immediately, a defeating thought went through my head, "You don't have time for any reading." I knew the thought came from Satan. With vindication and urgency, I grabbed my Bible and turned to the Book of Psalms, which is always my go-to book for inspiration and encouragement. However, my interest was captivated by the yellow, green, and pink highlights over the scriptures, and I decided to let my eyes follow the highlights. Those colorful lines led me on a journey to Isaiah 54. Suddenly, it was as if I was reading the words for the first time. The words of the passage spoke to me the answer to the question I had been asking: God: What is my purpose? What do you have for me to do? It became clear that God was telling me to finish a book I had started but abandoned. The book you hold today is that book.

For quite a while, I was struggling with getting another start at writing this book. Initially, God had given me this book idea in 2011 when I was going through a period of loneliness and stalled personal growth. I was in the midst of a struggle and with every decision I made I was sinking farther and farther into a pit of despair. It seemed like nothing was going right, and I couldn't seem to do anything right. It was a season in which I tried to support my husband, church, and family and neglected to care for my relationship with God and myself. My focus was so intense on others that I had forgotten about taking care of my personal needs. Though others around me were enjoying the positive benefits of my help, I was drowning in a murky pool of negativity.

If you listen carefully to the LORD your God and do what is right in his eyes, if you pay attention to his commands and keep all his decrees, I will not bring on you any of the diseases I brought on the Egyptians, for I am the LORD, who heals you.

Exodus 15:26

That moment reminded me that Satan's goal is to keep us so occupied and distracted by negativity that we can sometimes shift our focus away from the God who will never leave us nor forsake us. Whenever we are at the point that we get tired of struggling on our own and sick of living in defeat, discouragement, and disdain, we finally allow our focus to shift away from life's problems to the Problem Solver: God. Let's be real: Most of the time we spend too much energy focusing on what is happening to impact our lives negatively, instead of placing our concerns in God's hands. We need to acknowledge God for who He is: Jehovah Rapha—the Lord Your Healer.

In Isaiah 54, God spoke volumes of freedom, forgiveness, healing, encouragement, and redemption into my life. He did not want me to be afraid of how people would judge the content of the book, and He gave me peace and liberty to move forward with the details because I am forgiven and should not fear the judgment of others. We all have a story to tell; mine will be different from yours, but there are lessons that we can all learn.

At one point after writing the first and second drafts, I faded from writing and started enjoying being free and filled with God's amazing power. Then, there was a small whisper in my ear; "You've been healed. What about others?" God is a healer, and I pray that my testimony will help increase your faith that God's strength and mercy is able to help in times of struggles and hardships. When our focus shifts to God's promises and intentions for our lives, Satan cannot win. Now is the time to receive your strength, healing, and renewed passion for life.

As God continued to speak to me, He reminded me of three truths:

1. My past sins have been forgiven. "Come now, let us settle the matter," says the LORD. "Though your sins are like scarlet, they shall be as white as snow; though they are red as crimson, they shall be like wool" (Isaiah 1:18 emphasis added).

2. Do not be afraid of the judgment of people that will

occur behind closed doors, open places, and social media; "Do not judge, or you too will be judged" (Matthew 7:1).

3. And lastly, someone needs to read your testimony to be healed and take hold of the power of God and release the issues of the past. "They triumphed over him by the blood of the Lamb and by the word of their testimony; they did not love their lives so much as to shrink from death" (Revelation 12:11).

With those three reminders, I was back on track to completing this book. The passage in Isaiah 54 was my guide. God had given specific instructions in the chapter's verses that I believe will be a blessing for all of us. In this book I will share the following instructions that God shared with me:

- "Enlarge the place of your tent..." Stretch forth and trust that God is "able to do exceeding abundantly above all that we ask or think, according to the power that worketh in us" (Ephesians 3:20 KJV).
- "Do not hold back; lengthen your cords, strengthen your stakes"–Stretch yourself in order to reach the vision God has given you.
- "Spread out to the right and to the left"–Take the limits off of God.
- "You will forget the shame of your youth"–Your past is over!
- For your Maker is your husband–The Lord Almighty is His name.–I can't think of a better husband to have. He will supply all of your needs. He will protect you. He will love you. He will forgive you. He will not hold

anything against you. He won't remind you of your past. He will comfort you. He will guide you.

• "With everlasting kindness I will have compassion on you," says the Lord your Redeemer –The Lord will call you back as if you were a wife deserted and distressed in spirit. Although I turned and walked away, He was always present waiting on me to come back to Him.

And now is the time to come home to Him! My prayer is that this book will help lead you there.

Unfortunately, I know the consequences and struggles of turning away from God. For a brief moment God wasn't happy with the choices I was making, especially my willingness to stay in darkness. Yes! Anytime we are in darkness and don't seek God's face, we are willing to be in darkness. It is God's desire for His children to live in His beautiful light; in Him there is no darkness at all (1 John 1:5). He can turn your darkness into light. You are my lamp, O LORD; the LORD turns my darkness into light (2 Samuel 22:29). I am thankful that with everlasting kindness, He has compassion on me! As a father has compassion on his children, so the LORD has compassion on those who fear him (Psalm 103:13).

I open with Isaiah 54, because so many of us have lived in or are currently living in darkness. We have found ourselves lost in the wilderness and not on the path that was designed by Jehovah-Raah, our Shepherd, who tenderly leads us, loves us, and keeps us safe.

We do not have the right to allow our past and lack of forgiving others and ourselves to keep us from receiving healing and moving forward. Thinking on the past can stunt our ability to commune with God and yield to the Holy Spirit.

Fill the empty space and regrets you may have about the past by meditating on how you want to see things and make every effort to grasp the depth of God's love for you. Dwelling on a past that is not going to change is useless. That energy and time can be used to help someone else not go through the same things you've experienced. The past can be used as a stepping stone and should not be kept in our thoughts as a stumbling block. Step out on faith and trust in Jehovah Shammah, the One who is with us everywhere, because He is omnipresent.

Be strong and courageous. Do not be afraid or terrified because of them, for the Lord your God goes with you; he will never leave you nor forsake you.

Deuteronomy 31:6

Monica DeBro

Part One

Love the Lord your God with all your heart and with all your soul and with all your mind.

Matthew 22:37

In the first part of this book, I will address the broken relationship between God and me. Jesus said the greatest commandment was for all believers to love God the Father with all of our heart, soul, and mind. In order for every other relationship in a believer's life to function in victory, the relationship with the heavenly Father must be restored, sustained, and increased.

Monica DeBro

Chapter One:

Waging War

"It wasn't meant for you to remember."

Therefore, since we are surrounded by such a great cloud of witnesses, let us throw off everything that hinders and the sin that so easily entangles. And let us run with perseverance the race marked out for us, fixing our eyes on Jesus, the pioneer and perfecter of faith. For the joy set before Him He endured the cross, scorning its shame, and sat down at the right hand of the throne of God. Consider Him who endured such opposition from sinners, so that you will not grow weary and lose heart.

Hebrews 12:1-3

My Elements of Health and Wellness course at the University of Phoenix was coming to an end with the fifth night of class in March 2011. The students in the course were an enthusiastic group, and I looked forward to working with them every week on the assigned topics. Little did they know, I was battling with the daily struggle to live while fighting the demonic spirit of suicide that constantly plagued my mind. However, I wanted to finish my commitment to the university and to the students so that it would not affect their grades and the outcome of the course. At the same time that I was preparing to finish the last class, I was also preparing to bring my life to an end. My intent was to commit suicide and not have to deal with my inner pain and struggles. I respected the students enough not to cause them to have to deal with an instructor who took her life while at the same time teaching them how to overcome life's struggles and live their lives to the fullest. Looking back, my thoughts and teachings were definitely along the lines of the saying, "Do as I say, not as I do."

Have you ever been in a position of encouraging and teaching others and realized that you needed to take your own advice? How many times has someone come to you with an issue and you were able to give insight on how to deal with their situation while at the same time not adhering to what you've encouraged? A difficult thing to do is encourage and teach others when your life is in ruins, but to get through it we learn how to put up a good smokescreen of pretending that all is well, especially women. Somehow as women we find the strength needed to help others in spite of personal difficulties.

We need to take time to acknowledge our pain and seek help from a Christian woman. If you do not have a prayer partner, now is the time to pray and ask God to place someone on your heart who will be dedicated to pray with you and for you.

It was a struggle to complete the last class, which did not end until 10pm. The students were doing team presentations on various topics. Surprisingly, I was able to keep focused on their presentations in order to provide them with an accurate assessment and final score. As they finished their presentations, I immediately posted the rubric with comments and final scores into the grading system. After class, several of us stayed in the room to talk and said our well wishes before campus security asked us to vacate the premises so they could lock up the building.

I gathered my things, looked at the empty room, and thought about all of the laughs and tears we shared during the course. Walking through the parking lot to my car, I saw a symbolic reflection of how I was feeling on a daily basis: empty and dark with a flicker of light left within me. Sitting in the car, there was no hesitation as I popped 20 milligrams (mg) of a prescription sleeping pill into my mouth. I reasoned to myself, "Taking 20mg instead of my usual 5-10mg would surely put me to sleep quickly while I'm driving home." Normally, taking 5 to 10mg of sleeping pills at home before going to bed would put me to sleep within a few minutes. It was fast acting, which is why I chose it as the method to drift into a dark, sleepy death.

This will seem reckless, uncaring, unprofessional, and demonstrate a lack of thoughtfulness for others who were driving that night, but at the time, I did not think about the wellbeing of others. My suicide plan was to have a fatal wreck while driving. Thankfully, the drive home did not fulfill my plan and was uneventful. In fact, most of the details of my drive home that night are as clear as crystal. From that drive I remember seeing each landmark that would indicate how much longer I had to drive home: In-and-Out Burger, K-Mart, Castles and Coasters, and QuikTrip. I remember driving through the I-17 and I-10 curve, and the closer I got to my home, the more I realized the medicine was not taking affect.

One of the side effects from taking the sleeping pills is not remembering events and conversations. For example, you don't remember eating food but you see the evidence of wrappers and plates on your nightstand and crumbs in the bed. You may not remember a conversation with someone who called or even having sex with your spouse. This further increased the confusion on why I could remember specifics about the drive home. What I didn't realize at the time was that God had a purpose for me to remember the drive.

As I neared home, I started wondering, "Now what am I going to do? I'll be home in a few minutes with an unsuccessful initial plan." At that point, I should have been thinking, "OK Lord, you have another plan for me. Please show me what it is." But with blinders on and in deep depression, I felt like there was no point in living each day like a robot without any purpose for my life. I believed suicide was the best way to deal with it. I did not have a desire to focus on the future and did not see the need for forward thinking.

So I concocted plan B. If I was to make it home, I was going to stay in the car with it running and the garage door down. "Yes, that would be perfect. Relax, allow the medicine to take full effect and just go to sleep," I thought to myself.

"Besides, my husband wouldn't be awake to check on me. He's never awake after I get home from a 16-hour work day." It is interesting that I remember the 25-minute drive home, but not driving into the garage and getting out of the car. I don't remember gathering my purse and work bag from the car, opening the door and walking half way up the steps. If my second-ex-husband hadn't rolled over at around 2:30am and realized that I was not in the bed, I probably would have slept on the steps until later in the morning.

As I reflected on these past events when writing this chapter, God whispered to me, "It wasn't meant for you to remember." Had I remembered driving into the garage, I would have been cognizant enough to allow the garage door to fully close, keep the car running, lay the driver's seat back, become completely relaxed and allow the divisive plan of the devil to take its full course. God kept me alive that night, not anyone else, and it was His ultimate plan for me to live and not die. For that, I am grateful. Even in situations of our recklessness, God's will is going to be done.

I had no idea why God spared my life until He gave me the second part of the title to this book. I was a broken vessel and of little use for the Kingdom, but God said. "No more." No longer was I to be broken and weak. No longer was I to walk around with small cracks that were on the verge of rupturing. It was time to allow the ultimate Potter to place the broken pieces of my life back on the wheel to be molded and to have added usefulness for His glory. But it took more time before I allowed Him to heal me and mold me.

Having pride, I did not seek help for the suicidal thoughts and ideation until 2012 because I did not want anyone to know what had happened. I wasn't ashamed; I just didn't want people "all up in my business." You know how we can get when it comes to private matters. Because I was a leader in the church, there was an expectation for me to be a "strong woman of faith." Sometimes people fail to realize that a pastor and his wife are real people who face similar real-life situations as their congregation. It wasn't until I was continuously plagued with thoughts of suicide that I finally relented and sought outside help and started to become transparent about my feelings.

Depression and suicidal ideation are illnesses that can be overcome through fasting, prayer, studying God's Word, counseling, an effective treatment plan, and refocusing. People who do not understand the bondage of suicidal thoughts and the emotional struggles are not the best options to seek help from if you or someone you know is overwhelmed in the battle between choosing life and death. As a result, you may need to speak to someone other than your best friend, sister, or husband.

Although my ex-husband was a pastor, he was not supportive in what I was going through. Even after revealing the suicide attempt to him a couple of days after it happened, he had a negative demeanor. I remember him telling me, "You always talk about suicide." Not once did he say, "We need to get you help through counseling or I need to pray over you." Talk about a lonely feeling. When the one person I should be able to count on offered no support at all, it was damaging to my spiritual, emotional, and mental well-being. It was hard watching him be a support person, comforter, and helper for others in the church and fail to do the same with me, his wife. With this, my heartbreak continued and I plummeted further into depression. One of the signs of a person contemplating suicide is talking about suicide. No matter how many times a person makes a threat, it should be taken seriously.

It was not until much later that I thought about what would have happened if I had wrecked and been severely injured with multiple disabilities. Also, there was the unfortunate risk of causing harm to another family. It hurts my heart as I write this to think about the other consequences my actions could have had on others. There was a risk to not only my life ending in a fatal accident, but a risk as well of me causing the fatality of another person's life, and I sincerely apologize to everyone who was driving Interstate 17 North on March 30, 2011.

According to the Centers for Disease Control (CDC), the number of deaths caused by suicide is greater than the number of deaths caused by motor vehicle accidents. The most recent data from the CDC indicates that motor vehicle accidents accounted for 33,804 deaths, whereas the suicide rate was 41,149. This is 7,345 more deaths of people who took their own lives. If you are considering harming yourself, please do not suffer and try to hide your feelings. There are people trained to help you. The National Suicide Prevention Hotline number is 1-800-273-8255 and people are available 24 hours a day seven days a week to help.

We must identify depression, acknowledge thoughts of suicide, and seek professional help. Your place of employment may have a program to help with personal needs, or you may have a Christian mentor that you trust and feel confident that he or she will provide you with sound advice—Christian advice. If you do not have a mentor or prayer partner, pray and ask God to identify someone whom you can be accountable to who will pray with and for you.

Win the Battle with God's Weapons

After God supernaturally rescued me from my suicide attempt, I realized how Satan had launched an attack on my life. I chose to fight back with God's Word. Reading the Bible gave me strength, especially reading the personal journeys of Joseph and Job. I believe their ability to overcome will encourage you, too.

I found that I could relate to Joseph and his life story as told in Genesis chapters 37 and 39-45. When I considered the life of this 17-year-old young man, I recognized that like him I had dreams placed in my heart by God. Also, like Joseph, those closest to me chose to inadvertently plot out scenarios that would cause a change of events other than what was planned for my life. Joseph's jealous brothers schemed to kill him, but chose instead to sell him into slavery. While my second former husband did not plot my death, he betrayed my heart by not offering the support I needed when I was at my lowest point.

Despite the destructive actions of his brothers, Joseph still managed to thrive no matter where he was. When Joseph was placed in Potiphar's house, he was put in charge of the entire household and entrusted with everything Potiphar owned. Even when Potiphar's wife falsely accused Joseph of sexual misconduct and he was thrown into prison, Joseph still rose into leadership. The scriptures state, "The Lord was with Joseph..." (Gen. 39:2, 21). God demonstrated prosperity, kindness, and favor on Joseph's behalf, because despite how wrongly treated Joseph was, Joseph remained a servant to others and faithful to

God. Even after interpreting a dream for Pharaoh's imprisoned baker and cupbearer, the cupbearer forgot his promise to help Joseph get released from prison (Gen. 40:23). There may have been times when your kindness toward others was quickly forgotten. "And whatever you do, whether in word or deed, do it all in the name of the Lord Jesus, giving thanks to God the Father through him" (Colossians 3:17). We shouldn't do a kind act to be seen or to receive praise. Responding the way Joseph did when his kindness was forgotten will help us to focus on God rather than on the person.

Although Joseph faced numerous adversities, he remained faithful and was greatly favored with the Lord. Joseph's God-given destiny appeared to be altered or disrupted by people's actions toward him. However, although Joseph was a slave and wrongly accused and sent to prison, he continued to trust God, and Joseph's spirit did not change towards helping others. Joseph continued to provide his best as a servant of God regardless of the current situation. Joseph kept the vision in his heart and believed in the promises revealed to him in his dreams. A critical lesson to take from Joseph's trials and triumph is to remain faithful even when the dream seems to be moving further away. Don't ever give up, especially when things seem to be imperfect, out of range, and not in line with how you envisioned the situation. God has a plan. Keep the hope and stay encouraged. The outcome will be better than you ever imagined!

Another lesson for us is to not allow what we left in the past hinder our progress and blot out our dreams. If you notice, at no point in the Bible do we read about Joseph complaining or having a pity party. Imagine if Joseph had given up and only focused on how much his brothers disliked him or how Potiphar's wife lied about him or how the cupbearer forgot him. Joseph might have never fulfilled the dream God gave him. Joseph's providence and provision was interrupted, but he remained on course for his purpose. We must do the same.

Another biblical story to inspire you to keep moving forward is about Job. The Bible describes Job by saying, "This man was blameless and upright; he feared God and shunned evil" (Job 1:1b). Job was a family man who had many riches. Within a short period of time, Job lost everything: seven sons, three daughters, numerous servants, and all of his livestock. When you read the scripture, you will notice that while one of the servants was giving Job bad news another servant would arrive and inform Job of a different loss. But Job remained faithful: "In all this, Job did not sin by charging God with wrongdoing" (Job 1:22 NIV). How have you handled previous losses or stressful situations and events? Did they come back-to-back like Job's or spaced out? Did you find yourself blaming God?

When this did not work and Satan was not satisfied, Satan went back to God asking to continue to cause harm to Job. The Lord said to Satan, "Very well, then, he is in your hands; but you must spare his life. So Satan went out from the presence of the Lord and afflicted Job with painful sores from the soles of his feet to the crown of his head" (Job 2:6-7). Job remained faithful and did not curse God as Satan desired for him to do. Surprisingly, Job's wife told Job to give up. Actually, she told Job to curse God and die. "His wife said to him, are you still maintaining your integrity? Curse God and die!" (Job 2:9). How unfortunate for her to give up instead of having the compassion to pray for her husband! She obviously did not understand the healing power of God and the benefit of Job's suffering. There was a need for her to understand that God was allowing these things to happen and that God is always in control. Be patient with the internal and external work of God. He knows the end from the beginning (Isaiah 46:10).

Hearing what was going on with Job, his friends decided to visit. For the first seven days they sat in silence. Hmm! How many times have you sat in silence with a friend instead of giving unwelcomed and unnecessary advice? We don't always need to speak to provide comfort to others.

Throughout all of the hurt and pain, nothing in the Word indicates that Joseph and Job thought of committing suicide in the midst of their hardships. Even with the emotional, mental, and physical pain they were experiencing, suicide was not mentioned as an option for a way out. We need to have a Joseph and Job mentality when Satan attacks us with thoughts of self-harm. We need to have a Joseph and Job mentality to continue to magnify God, serve one another, and trust that He will continue to develop us into the women we are designed to be. Even when people try to put a stop to a God-given dream, God will give you the strength needed to ignore the naysayers and be prepared for when the opportunity arises. If we give up, we will never experience God's plans for our lives.

Jeremiah 29:11 states, "For I know the plans I have for you," declares the Lord, "plans to prosper you and not to harm you, plans to give you hope and a future." I understand that it gets hard, and we find it difficult to continue and deal with the issues of life. However, we will not reach God's ultimate plan and receive hope if we give up and allow Satan to win. Again, I urge you to seek help if you are contemplating suicide, because it is not a part of God's plan for your life.

Call on the name of Jesus when Satan attacks because there is unmatchable power in Jesus' name. "The name of the LORD is a fortified tower; the righteous run to it and are safe" (Proverbs 18:10). Speak the name of Jesus over your life every day. Speak the name of Jesus over thoughts of suicide. Use His Name to be freed from the controlling lies that Satan tells you. Satan is a thief and attempts to rob us of things that do not belong to him, including mental stability. There is no stability in Satan. If we accept what he has and give him what belongs to us, then instability happens. Satan takes; God gives. We are God's daughters and are worthy of the destination designed just for us.

We have to be prepared when Satan attacks and show him we have a bigger God than the situation. It is our responsibility to be prepared and recognize Satan's attacks. We have the weapons of fasting, praying, studying God's Word, the shed blood of Jesus, the word of our testimony, and agape love at our disposal to fight against the attacks of Satan. "For our struggle is not against flesh and blood, but against the rulers, against the authorities, against the powers of this dark world and against the spiritual forces of evil in the heavenly realms" (Ephesians 6:12).

The best weapon is speaking the Word of God over your life. When Satan attempts to interject negative words into your spirit, immediately rebuttal with a scripture. Then, rejoice and know there is victory over the devil. Christ suffered on the cross for us to have victory, redemption, and forgiveness of sin. "I have given you authority to overcome all the power of the enemy; nothing will harm you" (Luke 10:19).

In order to speak the Word, you have to have it available. Each person will find his or her own method of keeping the Word of God readily available to use as a weapon. When we speak God's Word, we bring God into our battle. His presence and His angels come on the scene when we speak the Word. If Satan has you in a dark place, pulling the strength together to fight against him can seem impossible. James 4:8 tells us to "Come near to God and he will come near to you; wash your hands, you sinners, and purify your hearts, you double-minded." If you are in a place where Satan has you feeling as though you cannot move forward or that the situation is greater than what it is, draw closer to God and Satan will flee. The devil has no power over you.

Having scripture cards readily available is a great way to keep God's Word close at hand. Psalm 119:11 says, "I have hidden Your Word in my heart that I might not sin against you." I know the skeptic may say that scripture cards are not needed, because we are to keep God's Word hidden in our hearts. However, Satan can have a stronghold on any individual that cannot "pull it together" to remember a scripture to speak over his or her life. Having the cards will allow you to speak out loud to combat Satan's attacks. It is not good enough to read them in our minds; we have to speak God's Word aloud to disarm Satan's schemes.

Using the weapons of praying and having a steady stream of praise and worship music to revive our spirits will help when we find ourselves thrust in the midst of an unsettled spirit. When you have a need–a great need for healing, preparation, and understanding for the next step God has planned for your life—pray and spend quality quiet time with Him. God's Word is clear: "Pray without ceasing" (1 Thessalonians 5:17 KJV). We need to be in constant prayer throughout the day. Our day needs to start with quiet time in prayer with God. It is surprising how many hours a day people will spend communicating with others through various devices, but spend little time communicating with God through simply speaking with Him. We can communicate with God without the need of technology and having to remember a password! Because there are numerous demonic spirits that can come into our environment, we need to pray for God's protection at the start of the day as well as throughout the day against the powers of darkness. Pray for discernment and trust God to answer prayers.

It is impossible to remain in darkness when we relent by giving glory to God and allowing Him to lead us in every way. Praying continuously and listening to praise and worship music throughout the day can help keep negative thoughts and emotions from clouding your judgment. Refuse to allow Satan to have dominion over any part of your day. Because of technology, there are several options to access praise and worship music. Filling the atmosphere with praise and worship music can help settle your spirit to be able to hear from God.

Chapter Two:
Hearing from God

Life had gotten so busy that I could not hear from God. My schedule was packed with meetings, work, church, and social activities. Nothing in my daily planning included personal time for spiritual growth. My day-to-day was also filled with continuous hours of unproductive activity. I had to learn the importance of turning off distractions, such as the reality television shows, which actually are not true reality. God cannot speak to us when distractions take priority over Him. Reality television has become a major distraction for many people: believers and nonbelievers. There are people who can tell you everything that is going on in reality television or soap operas, but they cannot recite John 3:16: "For God so loved the world that he gave his one and only Son, that whoever believes in him shall not perish but have eternal life." It is sad, but true. What is consuming your focus and preventing you from hearing from God? What does God think about those things that take our focus off of Him and what He has instructed us to do?

I encourage you to take purposeful action to hear from God. The primary way in which I did this was to create a dedicated space in my home to spend intimate time with God.

It meant so much for me to hear from God that I gave Him a whole room! Although, you may not be able to dedicate an entire room, find an area or space where you can make it a priority to meet with God every day. In my home I have a spare bedroom that I converted into a prayer room that I devoted to my special time with God. The room conversion took two years, because I would start decorating it and Satan would attack. My thinking was that it had to be "just right" before I started using the room for its intended purpose. But God wasn't concerned with human perfection and decorations; He simply wanted me to sit at His feet. I had a Mary heart in a Martha world (Luke 10:38-42). I was so busy with the work of creating the room that I lost the focus of its true purpose of needing a quiet space. One day I was talking to my counselor about the prayer room, she responded that Satan knew that having a dedicated place to meet with God would decrease his hold on my life. Satan would not have any strength to stand and would definitely not be welcomed into this area. Not that any of us welcome Satan in any area of our homes, but it is something about a special place for you and God. After talking to her I decided to be in the prayer room, decorated or not and this shift proved essential in how I started to hear from God. During the times when I knew that Satan was attacking me and I had no peace in my heart, I would spend my nights in the prayer room to receive solace.

This room was truly a dedicated space. Without realizing it, I had made an unconscious decision not to wear shoes in the prayer room. A couple of times when I was rushing off to work and needed to get something off the desk, I had worn my shoes into the room. I felt uneasy about it and after a couple of times of this happening, I whispered a simple question to God, "Why do I feel uneasy?" His immediate, simple reply: "The place where you stand is Holy ground." I was blown away at God's reminder that I had dedicated the room to Him and that He acknowledged it as holy. Needless to say, I have never worn shoes in the prayer room again.

Hearing From God Workout Plan

How many people do you know that will do everything in their power to remain physically fit, but fail to place the same importance on being spiritually healthy? They will get up early in the morning to go to the gym or jog in the park, but won't spend any energy on the spiritual aspect of their lives. They will spend numerous hours to make sure the physical body is in great shape. They are either working out to maintain their physical appearance or trying to lose weight. Choosing to be physically fit is a great way to maintain God's temple. However, we must take more time preparing our spiritual health. And that means exercising our ability to hear from God.

Now faith is confidence in what we hope for and assurance about what we do not see.

Hebrews 11:1

Consider if something was to happen to our physical health. If our spiritual health is intact, then we will have the faith that God will heal us physically. We need to be prepared for when there is an attack on another part of our health that requires spiritual strength and faith.

At a rapid pace, individuals will start a workout program, but then they will quit because they aren't experiencing instant results. Some Christians respond the same way when it comes to hearing from God and strengthening their spiritual health. Just like it takes time to become physically healthy (especially if the individual has had years of bad habits of eating and not exercising), it will take time to build our "faith-comes-by-hearing" muscles. We cannot give up on reading our Bible and praying even if we do not see the instant results we desire. You cannot go from being in the world all of your life and expect to quote scriptures in one day or in one week in the same manner as others who have been studying God's Word for years. Be patient and consistent. It won't be long before you are able to speak several scriptures as a result of spending time studying the Word and hearing from God. Furthermore, it will take time to become the woman God intends for you to be; the woman God made you to be. A butterfly must go through transition to change from something that crawls on the ground to a beautiful, colorful butterfly. In 2 Corinthians 3:18 it states, "And we all, who with unveiled faces contemplate the Lord's glory, are being transformed into his image with ever-increasing glory, which comes from the Lord, who is the Spirit." As you adopt a consistent plan and lifestyle to hear from God, you will be transformed into His image.

Hearing Prepares for Battle

The first part of the following scripture tells us to be strong in the Lord and in His mighty power. It is dangerous to attempt to be strong outside of the Lord's power.

Finally, be strong in the Lord and in his mighty power. Put on the full armor of God, so that you can take your stand against the devil's schemes.

Ephesians 6:10-11

When we attempt to be strong in our own power, we are setting ourselves up for failure. God never intended for us to struggle. We struggle and fail because we are outside of the will of God. We are seeking our own desires and not His desires. Because our desire is to fulfill God's plan, we must take precautions to prevent excluding Him during the journey, which means we must seek Him first and be open to hearing from Him. When we take that time, we hear the specific steps we should take. By His power, He will lead and help us stand against Satan's schemes to kill, steal, and destroy us.

Although we don't start each day looking for a battle, we must be prepared with the full armor of God on at all times. Anytime that we are missing a part of the armor it allows for an opening for Satan to attack our thoughts, heart, actions, and character. Maintaining the characteristics of God should be very important to us, because we are His children. In order to maintain godly character and put on God's armor, we should make it priority to start our day with spending time with God and hearing Him in our spirit. If we fail to take time to hear from God, then we may lose a battle during our day and compromise how others see God in us.

Winning the battle includes how we treat the waitress, waiter, or cashier who may get an order wrong or hand us the wrong amount of change. We have to be careful with how we react to others even with the simplest transaction. We cannot disrespect others while at the same time demonstrate the character of being God's child. Satan is aware of our weaknesses—small and large. It is up to us to make corrections in those areas to be able to stand against his attacks. Those corrections come when we are hearing God's Word through the Bible or hearing instruction and encouragement from the Holy Ghost. We have to stand our ground against Satan's schemes and learn to fight instead of whining, giving in, complaining, questioning God, and walking around with a slothful spirit. Use your armor. What are you wearing it for? It is meant for protection and we have to stand in authority and use what God had graciously given His daughters to flourish in the Kingdom.

Satan has a way of twisting our motives and actions, but the Holy Spirit has a way of reminding us of what is most important. We can wake up early in the morning with a nudging from the Holy Spirit to spend time in prayer or in reading the Word of God, and we need to be obedient no matter how early it is in the morning. There was a time when I was more diligent to get up and exercise before going to work. One day as I was walking in the park, the Holy Spirit said to me, "You're getting physically fit, and your spiritual health is suffering." I was broken and needed a serious focus on fasting, praying, and studying my way back to God to receive a healing and become a whole vessel to make a difference in His

Kingdom and at this moment God gently reminded me that my focus was wrong of what was a priority.

A broken vessel has little to no value. Brokenness can result in not trusting in God and forgetting that He can mold us back into beautiful complete vessels that can be filled with His undeniable love.

I had to start seeking after God with urgency to begin the healing process and move forward with my life. There was a desire for healing, but little action to receive what I needed from God. In James 2:26, it states, "As the body without the spirit is dead, so faith without works is dead." When we are not living by the spirit, everything in our lives can be considered dead. We are going through the daily requirements of life and think we are being fulfilled; however, we can be spiritually dead and not in the will of God.

But seek first His kingdom and His righteousness, and all these things will be given to you as well.

Matthew 6:33

If you need something from God, you have to put the work into whatever you need whether it is spiritual, emotional, mental, and financial. The unfortunate part is that many women do not realize a need for healing in these areas. They are going through a self-imposed, self-fulfilled life without the most important factor: a true relationship with God.

All the devil needs is a nugget—a mustard seed-sized

thought—to place in our minds to get us off track from the will of God. Refuse to entertain these thoughts. If you allow Satan, he will nag at you with a small force that seems unbearable and continues to grow in your spirit and mind. Before you know it, you have allowed this nugget to wear you down and cause undue frustration.

There was a time when I thought I had it all together with a successful career, maintaining three places of employment, providing for my children and husband, and supporting the church through various departments. The truth is, working three jobs and staying busy does not indicate having it all together. I was pouring so much time and effort into others that I neglected to make sure my spiritual and emotional well-being was intact. Focusing on making sure everyone else was taken care of and happy caused me to simply go through the motions of my daily routine without any true feelings or emotions. With each new day, my vessel began to crack under the pressure.

I was continuously giving and doing for other people with little coming back to me in return. I am not meaning financial or material return, but receiving comfort and prayer from others to me. On numerous occasions, I was fasting over something in my home or church. One time a friend told me, "Sure, you go ahead and fast, because every time you do, I get blessed." At the time, I did not give her statement much thought, but when I reflected on it years later, I realized that I was covering someone dear to me in prayer but neglecting to focus on praying for me.

The darkness had covered me so much that I had given up on life. But at the same time I was always considering others. It was a strange feeling. I had given up on myself, but wanted to make sure others met their goals and weren't negatively affected by my inner feelings of sadness. I craved freedom from this bondage of despair.

In the previous chapter, I mentioned the importance of having a song in your heart. The song "Free" by Kierra Sheard helped me greatly. It is an excellent song to put in your spirit if you are wrestling with mental disparity, thoughts of suicide, and past hurts. When we are free mentally, we can be captured by what God wants from us. We can be set free from demons that attack us and generational curses that have caused our families too much unwanted and unnecessary pain. Please have a desire to be free and not remain in bondage or darkness. We don't have to be in bondage in our thoughts. Our minds need to be free to hear from God and give God true praise.

Monica DeBro

Chapter Three:
Unsettled Spirits

Any life decision that remains unsettled in your spirit is an indication that God disapproves.

If your spirit is not settled on a decision you have made for your life, it may not be in God's plan. Have you put your trust in Him and sought Him through prayer? Proverbs 3:5-6 states, "Trust in the Lord with all your heart and lean not on your own understanding; in all your ways submit to him, and he will make your paths straight." This scripture should be applied to every decision we are facing in our lives. As mentioned in the previous chapter, by hearing from God we know that we will receive clear directions.

I have had a strong desire to obtain my doctorate degree and had attempted to complete a doctoral program on three different occasions. During the first program, I was going to school to earn a doctorate in education. Sadly, I was bored and unfulfilled with the coursework. I participated in the discussion questions and completed the papers and team assignments. However, my interest level was sub par, and it was hard to focus and remain motivated.

The second program I applied to was for a doctorate in counseling. While it was interesting, I realized that I needed a previous background in counseling to be successful at the doctorate level. For the third attempt, I applied for a doctorate of nursing at Arizona State University (ASU) that began in the fall of 2012. I was in a great position to be selected for the program. However, my spirit was not settled with the idea of returning to school and having to spend numerous hours researching, answering discussion questions, writing papers, and taking exams. Although I knew I could handle going to school, because I had been successful in my master's degree program, there was a constant nudge that it was not the right time to return to school.

I prayed about attending school and sought God's guidance on my desire to start school. After several weeks, there was an uneasy feeling about my decision to return to school. With my senses and spirit in an uproar, it must not have been in God's plan at that time. After calling the nursing department at ASU to withdraw from the selection process, there was a complete covering of relief.

It was not until January 2013 that the Holy Spirit revealed to me the reason it was not yet the time to pursue a doctorate degree. During what would have been my fall semester in 2012, I encountered numerous changes in my life: Both of my parents passed away and my divorce was finalized. My mother passed away on September 1 and my father joined her in Heaven on November 6. The following month my divorce was finalized. Imagine if I had continued pursuing my natural desires instead of understanding and yielding to God's nudging that now was not the time. I would have been in more debt and had another unsuccessful attempt at a doctorate degree.

God always attempts to shield us from failure. Unfortunately, there are times when we want to see with the natural eye and not the heart. This can cause unnecessary pain, failure, rejection, and turmoil that could have been prevented by listening to the Holy Spirit. Don't keep knocking on a door that was meant to be closed. If you force your way through, the end result won't be one that you're expecting because it was not ordained by God.

My grace is sufficient for you, for my power is made perfect in weakness.

2 Corinthians 12:9

God has a plan for us and we must be patient because He will give us what we need at just the right time.

I am thankful for God's grace and mercy over my life. There have been numerous bad decisions and unnecessary suffering in my life because of poor decisions and unhealthy thought processes and actions. His grace has protected me; His blood has cleansed me; and His mercy has saved me. My life has been spared, because God loves me and wants the best for me. God's love will move us from darkness into His marvelous light. Don't hurt the Father's heart by remaining in an area of darkness with an unsettled spirit. It is not His will or desire for believers to be in the wilderness.

Have you ever been in a position where you are living in darkness and nobody can see it? You are going through the motions simply because it is required. Deep down inside you are hurting and crying out for help. No one can recognize the pain, because you've learned how to disguise your true feelings. You may have sought help only to be let down. It is important to remember God as Jehovah-Shammah: the One who is with us everywhere for He is omnipresent. He is always with us, and this should reassure us that He sees everything and knows exactly when we are hurting. Our job is to seek after Him with everything we have to prevent Satan from pulling us further into despair.

But you are a chosen people, a royal priesthood, a holy nation, God's special possession, that you may declare the praises of Him who called you out of darkness into His wonderful light.

1 Peter 2:9 NIV

God is the only one who can bring us from darkness into the life He pre-ordained for us. Our responsibility is to seek His help and be prepared to make any changes needed to live in His light. We cannot live in darkness and light at the same time. Talk about an unsettled spirit. Darkness and light don't blend together and cannot take up the same space. It is much easier to follow a lighted path than to try to find our way along a dark and deserted path.

While shifting from the pits of darkness, the timing seemed

right for me to take additional steps toward professional growth. Obtaining a doctorate degree would increase my marketability in nursing education. It would definitely be a highlight in my portfolio and open opportunities for growth and a teaching position at the university level.

As if the previous three attempts were not enough, in May 2013, I was introduced to American Sentinel University, which offered a Doctorate of Nursing Practice in Educational Leadership. After calling the university and obtaining information about the admission requirements, program expectations, and online requirements for posting to discussion questions, course lengths, and breaks between courses, it seemed to be a manageable program. The degree would be completed in two years and a dissertation was not required. To hold my place for a seat in the October cohort, I needed to pay a $2,500 placement fee by mid-August of 2013.

I was excited, ready to get started, and at peace for about 12-hours with the decision to return to school in October. Going back to school would speed up the timeline for completing the book, and I acknowledged and accepted this truth. However, the next day while at work, something was different, and I was unsettled in my spirit, again. Not knowing what was going on, I prayed and proceeded with my day as usual. Later in the evening, as I was driving to my local church for midweek service, I started praying again and asking God to reveal why I was feeling uneasy. He revealed to me once again that it was not the right time to go back to school. Accepting His answer, I had immediate relief and called my friend to inform her that I was not going to apply for the school. This was a true revelation that my timing is insignificant to God's timing.

Months later God whispered to me that I could not apply for school until I finished the book and that I would not have to pay tuition for my doctoral degree. On February 21, 2014, I received an email from an admissions representative that I was eligible for 100% paid tuition for a Doctorate of Nursing Practice degree. My financial responsibility would include the $60 application fee, $600 student service fees per session, and books. All the glory belongs to God. Hallelujah!

Sometimes we can have a dream and desire that is pulling at us so hard that we want to consistently knock on a door that is not ready or should not be opened. Proverbs 16:1-3 states, "To humans belong the plans of the heart, but from the Lord comes the proper answer of the tongue. All a person's ways seem pure to them, but motives are weighed by the Lord. Commit to the Lord whatever you do, and He will establish your plans." God knew the desires of my heart and at the appropriate time He guided me into the blessing of applying for school to obtain a doctoral degree. He has made it so plain that I know that it is God who has opened the door.

Give thanks to the LORD, for he is good; his love endures forever.

1 Chronicles 16:34

The key to any decision is to pray and ask God for guidance. When we have an unsettled spirit, we should seek Him first before jumping into any situation that will not benefit our lives and cause us to have regrets, destroy relationships, and incur financial debt. God already knows our hearts and desires, so it is best that we are honest in our prayers and place clear definition and description of what we are seeking. God will answer prayers. It may not be the desired answer we are seeking, but there will be an answer.

Look for subtle signs to the answers to your prayers. God's answers are not always with thunder, lightning, shaking and

"For I know the plans I have for you," declares the Lord, "plans to prosper you and not to harm you, plans to give you hope and a future."

Jeremiah 29:11

moving of the earth. The door is not always a slam in our face, but it can be a gentle closing when God does not want us to go down a certain path. If there is any dimness on the path, keep seeking the right direction. When God gives an answer of "yes" to move forward or "no" to yield and stop, just know and believe in your heart that He has given the right answer.

God will answer our prayers whether we are in the prayer closet or driving down a bustling highway. No matter where we are, we can hear His voice. Although I have a prayer room at home, I have awesome quiet times of prayer and praise and worship with God in the car. This quiet time with God has been intense moments with an outpouring of the Holy Spirit. Always be available to pray for yourself, family, pastor, church, friends or anyone who has rested on your heart. You may never know why you were led to pray but Jehovah-Nissi—our banner, a banner of love and protection—knows exactly why you needed to intercede with prayer.

Have you heard the acronym PUSH, which stands for pray until something happens? It's a good saying, but truthfully, we should do more than pray until something happens. We should act on faith, because faith requires work. We can pray and have faith, but if we are not placing actions on what we are praying for it will have little to no results. Action must be attached to faith in order to meet goals, dreams, and the daily tasks of life. It is useless to sit around doing nothing and expect productivity and positive answers to prayers. We need to prepare ourselves so that when God answers the prayer we are ready to move forward instead of saying, "OK, I need to get it together now that God has answered my prayer." God is more likely to answer a prepared person's petition than someone who is just sitting and waiting.

If your spirit is not settled about a person in your life, examine his or her qualities. What is it about the person that makes you feel uncomfortable? Are they always filled with negative conversation and never have anything good to say? Maybe the person brings negative energy into the room and everyone knows that the smallest thing will set him or her off. What adjustments are you willing to take regarding the individual? It's important to take time to pray and hear from God about if you should be in relationship with the person.

We have to be aware of the company we keep. God mentions who we should stay away from in scripture: People will be lovers of themselves, lovers of money, boastful, proud, abusive, disobedient to their parents, ungrateful, unholy, without love, unforgiving, slanderous, without self-control, brutal, not lovers of the good, treacherous, rash, conceited, lovers of pleasure rather than lovers of God—having a form of godliness but denying its power. Have nothing to do with such people. They are the kind who worm their way into homes and gain control over gullible women, who are loaded down with sins and are swayed by all kinds of evil desires, always learning but never able to come to a knowledge of the truth (2 Timothy 3:1-7). This scripture is full of characteristics that we should not have as daughters of God. It is critical that we are mindful of the people we allow in our lives and into our homes.

People who are unhappy with who they are have become determined to make everyone around them unhappy as well. Do not allow people to take your joy away and avoid people who have a bullying and undermining spirit. Negativity can cause an immediate shift in the atmosphere, which can be draining if you have to spend time with the person.

Having the negative characteristics described in the scripture above can destroy relationships—personal and professional. When you begin to recognize that you're having difficulty with people, the problem may not be everybody else. You may need to do a self-check. If people are avoiding spending time with you ask a friend if they have noticed any of these characteristics in you. Be open to honest constructive criticism. Leave the hard-heartedness at the door because there is no room for it when doing a self-check.

Ask a friend to give you an honest assessment of your daily character by giving you examples of how you to tend to respond in various situations. For instance, you could ask your friend to observe your behavior and verbal responses when you are interacting with others and give your friend the freedom to be honest with you without the threat of repercussions. Questions to consider include:

- Do you easily tell people how you feel regardless of how it will make them feel?
- Do you shut down and avoid group interaction because someone offended you?
- Do you have a bullying spirit and use it as a way to make others feel uncomfortable because you're upset?
- Do you assess the whole situation or promptly blame others when things don't go your way?

I suggest you pray before having the assessment done and please don't be easily offended. I do not understand how adults are so easily offended and feelings get hurt when they are made aware of a behavior that needs to change. Correction is a necessary part of growing and maturing.

Ask God to open your heart to receive and take action toward improving the character weaknesses revealed to you. Once the character check is completed, say to yourself "I'm better than that" and pray that God will help you become as Genesis 1:27 describes us: "So God created mankind in His own image, in the image of God He created them; male and female He created them." We are made in the image of God and we can only change with His help. You can also ask the friend to hold you accountable whenever the bad character is displayed so that you can become more aware of your behavior.

If the negative characteristic begins to reveal itself, recognize what is causing the character and make a mental or written note of what "set you off." Identifying who and what causes us to have ungodly actions allows us the opportunity to avoid, as much as possible, the places, people, issues, and topics that negatively impact us. Sometimes we have to remove ourselves from people and places that we once enjoyed because we realize that they are a hindrance instead of a benefit to our lives.

Years ago, this same character assessment was performed on me. My dear friend pointed out that I demonstrated a negative characteristic of "going off" on people for no reason. Initially, I was taken back at the person having the nerve to make such a negative but necessary comment. As I began to observe my reactions to people, I was embarrassed and began to make immediate changes in how I responded to numerous situations. There were issues where I was making myself upset for nothing and probably causing the other person to think I was some crazy, bitter woman. Recognizing the negative spirit helped me to become more settled in how I treated others. Had I not been informed of my actions I would have kept thinking it was OK to tell people what I thought regardless of how their feelings may have been hurt or how I was appearing as a Christian woman.

We all need work in the character department! Hopefully there isn't anyone reading this who is honestly thinking, "I'm good; there's nothing wrong with me." Shame on you! We all have areas in our lives that need improvement and should be willing to be transformed into a better person. Here's an example. Have you ever hit the snooze button one time too many and stayed in bed longer than you should have? Maybe you didn't prepare for work the night before and found yourself running around the closet trying to figure out what to wear. On top of that, you forgot to wrap or roll your hair and have to take time to put a little heat to it in the morning. How is that going to affect your morning drive to work? Maybe you're not going to work but to church, dinner, a birthday party, or a concert. Are you going to be able to remain calm when the city has decided to do construction on one of the main streets? Maybe the interlinking freeway has been closed for maintenance. Is it really everyone else's fault because you're

But He gives us more grace. That is why Scripture says: "God opposes the proud but shows favor to the humble."

James 4:6

running late? Are you going to remain calm or will you have a few choice words to voice out at everyone? Now remember, they cannot hear you so who is really getting the brunt of your actions. Look in the rearview mirror for the answer. Preparing and leaving home on time will prevent you from having a negative, unsettled spirit and allow you to arrive at the destination without being frustrated. Don't make your lateness or laziness someone else's emergency when you made the personal decision to procrastinate.

Something as minor as hitting the snooze button can lead to an unsettled spirit because it can change the course of us having a peaceful start to the day. Hitting the snooze button can cause us to miss the opportunity to hearing something specific from God as a result of not committing the first part of our day to meet with Him. There is an easy fix, humbly admit that we need help, pray, and ask God to help us remove the poor habits that continue to occur in the same area of our lives as a result of not making necessary adjustments. An unsettled spirit is

Pride goes before destruction, a haughty spirit before a fall. Better to be lowly in spirit along with the oppressed than to share plunder with the proud.

Proverbs 16:18-19

God's way of letting us know that something is not quite right in our lives. Whether it's a person, situation, or the woman in the mirror, take the time to seek God in everything that you do and ask others to help you in your walk with Christ.

When you are not at peace with any decision you've made or direction that you're planning to take, ask God to guide you and provide the instructions that you need to be on course with His will for your life.

Chapter Four:

Living in God's Light

When a woman is living in darkness, her walk with God has faded. For quite some time, internally I was telling God that my issue was bigger than anything that He could handle. Subconsciously, it was as if I was telling God, "Never mind looking down on me; there is nothing that You can do to save me. Don't worry about trying to lift me up. I'll just wallow in the place where I am without accepting that You love me enough to save me from this encapsulated darkness that is surrounding my life."

Daughters of God, what gives us the right to tell God how to love and take care of us? As His daughters, we have rights, but this is not one of them. Get rid of the poor-me mentality, because it is not a good look. This mentality, if maintained for long periods of time, can actually drive people away from you. The poor-me attitude doesn't represent God's kingdom. We are not meant to be partakers of negativity, poor self-worth, or diminished self-esteem. Recognize the attacks of Satan on your thoughts and how he has implanted discouragement. Then, choose to change the course of your progress and path back toward God's light.

Merriam Webster's Dictionary defines discouragement as

the act of making something less likely to happen or of making people less likely to do something or a feeling of having lost hope or confidence. Discouragement will keep you from seeing the beauty of the day by making you think it is cloudy outside on a beautiful sunny day. Discouragement will change your outlook on life and keep you from pursuing the vision God has given you. Discouragement can ultimately make you want to take your life and miss the many blessings God has for you.

One of the best words I can think of to describe discouragement is plague. According to Free Online Dictionary, plague (verb) means to cause continual trouble or distress or to pester or annoy persistently or incessantly. Satan is a plague that can ultimately destroy a person's ability to be productive and constructive with daily tasks. Unfortunately, many people have missed the mark because they've been plagued by the spirit of discouragement. They aren't able to "press toward the prize for which God has called them heavenward in Christ Jesus" (Philippians 3:14). The plague of discouragement can ultimately affect a person's self-worth, self-confidence, and self-esteem to the point that she sees absolutely no hope for the future. If you want to get rid of that discouraging spirit, speak to it and tell it to leave you; don't ignore it and allow it to fester and grow.

Which fruit are you eating and speaking—life or death? Pay attention to the words you speak into the atmosphere. The words you speak impact whether or not you will live in God's light. If you're suffering with depression, start speaking words of healing over your mind and emotions. If you want a stronger relationship with God, you have to start praying, studying, and speaking the Word of God aloud. If you want your children to be respectful, obedient, and mindful of others (outside of not sparing the rod), pray and speak life into the children. Too many parents are verbalizing the negative behaviors of their children instead of speaking what they want their children to be. If you tell a child that he or she is bad, you are speaking it into existence and supporting Satan's desires for the child to be disobedient. Speak life and watch your family live in God's light!

The tongue has the power of life and death, and those who love it will eat its fruit.

Proverbs 18:21

What do you need from God? In what way do you need Him to move and release the daily pressures of life? Do you wake up in the morning with a gloom and doom outlook? Has Satan gotten on your last nerve with his constant attacks? It's time to speak up and speak life! Whatever you need to speak against, don't keep it bottled up inside of you. When Satan begins to attack our day, we need to speak biblical confessions into the atmosphere and stand boldly on God's Word. In James 4:7 it states, "Submit yourselves, then, to God. Resist the devil, and he will flee from you." Jehovah Shalom will give us perfect peace.

Call into existence the things that do not exist.

Romans 4:17

God wants us to live in His light and

experience life with abundant joy and thanksgiving. Spending time without joy is like telling God that He has done wrong by blessing you with another day. We didn't bring the day into existence through our own abilities and do not have the right not to enjoy it as God so ordained. "This is the day the LORD has made. Let us rejoice and be glad in it" (Psalm 118:24 ESV). Even when we think the day is going to be a challenge, which sometimes happens, acknowledge it and ask the Father to give you power to be productive and to bind up Satan's schemes.

Having dread for the day does not glorify God. Being fake about having joy is not glorifying God. Let's be real! We have fake tendencies even with praise and worship. If you say, "I've never done that," then think about a time when you went to church after trying to get your family ready and someone got on your last nerves just before service. Or if you're married to a pastor or minister and he had to preach after Satan snaked his way into the morning and caused friction between the two of you. You go to church, smile, shake hands, give hugs, and participate in praise and worship only because it was expected, but your heart was not in it. Were you really giving true worship? We have to push through whatever has taken our focus off of praising God and ask the Holy Spirit to overflow in us.

Living in God's light is about being real and sincere. God knows our innermost being and knows when we are giving Him true praise. There is nothing fake about our God. Imagine if your employer paid with fake checks or imagine the troubles the church would have if people paid tithes with Monopoly® money. On a side note, think about how people say they love God with all their heart but refuse to pay their tithes. God does not bless us with a half-hearted spirit, He is Jehovah Jireh; the Lord our Provider. He takes joy in blessing us and He is worthy of true worship.

Recognizing when Satan is on the prowl is a quality that all Christians need to have. Satan is constantly working against us and trying to persuade us to take a different route from living in God's light. The adversary is not sneaky but is bold in action and has no shame in the works he is doing. In John 10:10, Jesus explains Satan's objective: "The thief comes only to steal and kill and destroy." Regardless of how we feel about it, Satan is on attack 24 hours a day, seven days a week, 12 months a year. He is relentless in the pursuit to make us fail and turn away from God. As soldiers, we must have on the full armor of God, 24 hours a day, seven days a week, 12 months a year in order to resist and stand strong against Satan's attacks.

God is a spirit, and his worshipers must worship in the Spirit and in truth.

John 4:24

Are we going to live in darkness and allow Satan to steal, kill, and destroy our minds, actions, and love for God and ourselves? Or are we going to live in God's light where there is the fullness of His joy, peace, and happiness? Choose the latter. Jesus sacrificed so that we could live in the light. Jesus said in John 10:10, "I have come that they may have life, and have it to the full." How exciting! We have to decide who is going to have the victory in our lives. Always have an eagerness to live according to God's Word and receive the gifts He so earnestly wants to provide.

The devil does not deserve to steal our joy, dreams, visions, goals, families, jobs or anything God has promised us. Avoid allowing negativity to destroy you and put you in a box or in a corner. When we allow ourselves to be pushed into a box, we can literally be going about life emotionally disconnected. What do I mean by this? When you find yourself simply going through the motions of everyday life without having true meaning or feelings, you are emotionally disconnected. It's difficult to enjoy life without experiencing emotions and being discouraged from showing our emotions. Living in God's light indicates that we accept, trust, and love God and that we acknowledge that when we face trials and tribulations that He is the anchor that will keep us steady and prevent us from drifting. When we live in God's light, we exude happiness instead of hostility; we have a character of power and peace instead of pity; and we magnify unrelenting love instead of practicing unforgiveness. Accept the authority to live in God's light.

Part Two

Love your neighbor as yourself.

———◐◑———

Matthew 22:39

In the second half of this book, I will focus on the believers' relationships with others. Once we are in right standing and right fellowship with our heavenly Father, we have the grace and supernatural ability, to be in proper and right relationship with those around us.

Monica DeBro

Chapter Five:
Relationships

**"When the past calls, let it go to voicemail.
It has nothing new to say."**

– Unknown

Imagine the following scenarios:

Scenario 1: Two friends take a vacation to Mexico with plans to have a fun time and enjoy the sites. Friend A meets a man and starts having vacation sex with him. Friend B relaxes, enjoys her time, but doesn't involve herself in casual sex with a stranger. When it was time for the friends to return home, the man meets them at the airline gate and presents Friend A with a large card and instructs her not to open it until they are in the air. Joyfully, she accepts and accommodates to his wishes. Once the plane takes off, Friend A opens the card and reads the shocking message, "Welcome to the world of AIDS."

Scenario 2: A woman is in a relationship with a man that she knows has a "primary" girlfriend and that she is the "side chick." Initially, she considers it as being harmless fun and a way to escape her hectic week. They would drink and occasionally smoke marijuana. This woman is a Christian but has found herself in a situation that is against her beliefs. Her conflicting desire to live victoriously in Christ and stay in an uncommitted relationship was a constant tug-of-war with her heart. God started keeping her busy with work responsibilities, which kept her from being able to spend time with the man. After not seeing him for several weeks and having time to sort out her feelings, she realized that she did not want to be in the shadow of another woman when in a relationship. But another thought was nagging at her, which was making it easier for her to walk away. God kept whispering in her ear, "I'm sparing you, but if you continue to go against my will, I cannot protect you." She had suspected that he was having sex with multiple women, and ultimately God was pre-warning her to immediately terminate from the relationship to prevent a lifelong disease. Only God knows what the outcome would have been if she had not heeded His warning.

Unfortunately, women face these scenarios every day. The first scenario is one that was told to me more than 20 years ago, and the second one was a personal account. I will share more details about that period in my life in a later chapter. While an unsuspecting woman may not receive the large "going-away" card like Friend A in scenario 1, it is never easy to hear that she was diagnosed with human immunodeficiency virus (HIV). Working in the healthcare field, I unfortunately have witnessed firsthand the emotional devastation of women being diagnosed with HIV. The emotional strain has caused turmoil to these women. So much so that it is difficult for them to shift from the initial shock of learning about their diagnosis and progressing through the grief process.

The grief process not only occurs when there is a death of a loved one, but grief can be experienced when a person is given a negative health report, such as cancer or HIV. According to the Kübler Ross model, the five stages of grief are denial, anger, bargaining, depression, and acceptance (Kübler Ross Foundation). Denial involves not accepting the diagnosis or information that has been received, and the patient may think there has been an error in the testing.

Displaced anger at others as a result of accepting the diagnosis makes it difficult for the person to receive comfort from family and friends. The deep desire to have another chance and longer life indicates a shift to the bargaining stage: "Just let me live until … I will do better if…" Feelings of hopelessness can transition the person into depression and cause an "I give up" spirit. This lasts until the woman accepts reality and decides to move forward with her life. There are women who have become advocates and teach other women, young and old, about risk factors and the importance of protecting themselves.

There's overwhelming data regarding HIV that should increase our awareness on the prevalence of the disease. According to the U.S. Department of Health and Human Services:

- Every 9½ minutes, someone in the U.S. is infected with HIV. It is estimated that there are over 56,000 new cases of HIV in the U.S. each year.
- It is estimated that 1.7 million people in the U.S. have been infected with HIV since 1981 and approximately 1.1 million Americans are currently living with the infection.
- About one in five infected Americans doesn't know he or she has the virus.
- Nearly half of all new HIV infections occur in African

Americans, even though they comprise only about 12 percent of the U.S. population.

• Women account for a growing portion of individuals living with HIV in the U.S.—more than a quarter according to the Centers for Disease Control and Prevention. More than 180,000 women in the U.S. have HIV.

Unfortunately, many people have a "nothing is going to happen to me" attitude when it comes to having unprotected sex whether casual sex or marital affairs. In reality, there are men and women who are purposefully having unprotected sex with the sole purpose of infecting others. The purposeful intention of infecting others is a direct result of anger and revenge to hurt innocent people. "In many countries, intentionally or recklessly infecting another person with HIV is a crime. In the United States, the Center for HIV Law and Policy documented that 32 states and two territories—Guam and the U.S. Virgin Islands— have such laws on their books" (Young, S., 2012).

There are women who are committed to their marriages, only to be infected with HIV by their husbands who have been unfaithful with other women, and for some, other men. Some may have been devastated and unable to move forward and sought alcohol and drug use as a way of coping. Others, who were devastated and moved through the five stages of grief, turned to God for His dunamis power. Dunamis is the miraculous power of God that is able to bring a change in a person's life. Seeking God for the healing of their bodies, hearts, minds, emotions, and spirits is the best and only method to receive healing. Strength and comfort to deal with the stares and rejection from family will come from relying on God. Imagine the rejection someone feels when she reveals an HIV positive status. The fear of rejection can cause her to become isolated and withdrawn. Running to the strong tower of God provides the ability to stand and work through the rejection.

Consider the past and current intimate relationships you have had: Did you or have you committed yourself to a man who would not commit to you? This would be any woman who is in a relationship with a man who is married or openly informed you that he is in a relationship with another woman. He has blatantly informed you that he is committed in a relationship, but you ponder to yourself, "How committed can it be if you're spending time with me?" In no way will this situation apply to everyone reading this book, but let's be realistic, it is occurring more often than people are willing to admit. Having been in this situation before, I know that sometimes we think "I have fun with him. I enjoy his company. He's a great guy." Of course the overall verbalized quote is "But I love him." Whatever! As the saying goes, "been there, done that." We are placing ourselves in delusional and false-love relationships. The man is not going to leave his wife or woman to commit to someone else. And if he does, you will be on constant watch thinking that he is cheating on you.

It is an unemotional and detached relationship on his part. Think about it: The woman he is truly in a relationship with wants the same thing that you are seeking—a committed, lifelong, trusting relationship. He can't give you the desires of your heart because it is impossible to be in two committed relationships at one time. There won't be a commitment emotionally, spiritually, financially, or physically. If you have been or currently are in this type of relationship, you know this to be true. The questions that come along are "Is he with her? What are they doing? If he's not with her or me, where is he? Is he with someone else?"

Imagine being in a relationship with a man who is dating someone else. You have asked him to take you to an event that is coming up, and he continuously gives several excuses for why he will not take you. Finally, you decide to accept another invitation to the same event. Who did you run into? The man and his lady. Wouldn't that be enough of a wake-up call for you to walk away? This type of relationship places blinders on a woman and binds her spirit to be unable to receive true love. More importantly, it damages her relationship with the Father, the One who can give her true love. She won't be able to recognize when a genuine man is in her midst and ready to be a blessing to her life. She is caught up in a fog of never-ending hope for a relationship that will never be fulfilling. In a sad revelation, God's work cannot be done when we are caught up in false reality. Think about it: Why would He send a king, when a woman is in defiled territory?

I am not the one to point fingers. I have been in the hog's pen of relationships. Enjoying the "fun times" in a false reality until God spoke to me while I was in the midst of the mud and said, "Come home My child." There is a better life when living completely for God's kingdom. We should not lower our standards just to have a man who is not ordained to be in our lives. Be patient and wait on God to send the man that He has designed for your life. Your husband will fit into your life like a well-placed piece of the puzzle. It won't be a forced fit or a struggle to put all of the pieces together. Pray and ask God to open the man's eyes to see you, and your heart to receive his invitation for a godly relationship at the appropriate time.

Closed Doors

The week prior to my youngest son's high school graduation, I had been praying for God to show me a sign of whether his father and I would be able to mend our relationship and start over. I asked God to give me a sign that would be like no other sign and one that I would not question. You have to be careful what you pray for and be prepared for when God responds. The answer may come in a subtle method and others like a lightning bolt. God's answer to this request had a little bit both.

Generally, when I went to Louisiana, there would be some communication or connection from my first ex-husband. But this time was different. There wasn't a response to the text that I was in town and no attempt to contact me whatsoever. Reality check! Communication and contact with him would have clouded the events that followed later to solidify in my heart and mind the answer from God.

In the early morning hours, while it was cool and most people were still sleeping, I used that serene time to pray, listen to music, and read. The morning of my son's graduation I went by the pool to enjoy some quiet time. The water from the pool was glistening, a cool breeze filled the air, and from a distance the sounds of birds could be heard. Without any warning, God answered my prayer. The tears started to flow immediately followed by a simple prayer, in which I asked that He give me the strength to accept His answer. Suddenly, the quiet place seemed like somewhere I wanted to escape from, but I stayed still to continue to hear what was needed and what I had been waiting for.

Remember I said that you have to be careful what you pray for. I had asked God for a clear sign and because He knows me as His child, He knew I was hard headed. As we stood in line to enter the church for graduation, the line of people waiting to enter was getting long. I was being the dutiful mother and saving seats to make sure we all could sit together. Since my first ex-husband had not arrived, I asked his sister to text him to see how many seats he needed. The reply he gave was six. In my head I asked myself, "Why does he need six seats?" It's just him, his mom, and his mom's boyfriend. Without knowing it, I was also saving seats for my ex-husband, his current girlfriend, and her two children. Talk about a slap in the face. I was irritated at him and my son for not telling me that this was "going down." Thank God the graduation was in a church, because I was still in the "broken believer" state and could not react the way my mind wanted to and had to rely on God for strength.

Thank God I had the sense to walk out of the church to gather myself and then returned to the sanctuary to get my scripture cards out of my purse. Soon, the Word was pouring into my spirit. It took a while, but I finally calmed down through praying, reading scriptures, and let me not forget that I put my earplugs in to listen to worship music. I was using every source to connect to the Father. Thank God I remembered that the night was about my son, and I was not about to let anything change his experience or devalue his success. By the time graduation started, I was over it!

Now, God answered my prayer, but it did not mean that there wouldn't be some hurt to accompany the answer. Here is the interesting part about healing through the pain: I refused to allow the situation to put me back into a place of darkness. I refused to allow the situation to hinder my growth and relationship with God. God only did what I asked him to do, which was give an answer. We cannot become hardhearted about receiving answers to prayers when the answer is no. In less than a week, I was laughing about the situation.

The chuckles came as I was walking down the hall one day at clinical, the Holy Spirit quietly spoke to me and said, "not only did the door close, but it was slammed in your face." That may seem harsh, but it is reality. Sometimes the door has to be slammed in our face in order for us to move in the direction God wants us to go. Otherwise, we'll keep knocking on that door until our knuckles are raw. Or the door will be opened because of persistence and the consequences will have to be dealt with. Later in the day when the thought came to me again, I started laughing and thinking to myself, "You asked for it." From that point on, I moved forward and never looked back again. When should you let go of a relationship and move on? Does your situation reflect any of these?

1.   If the relationship is bringing you pain, it is not a part of your promise.
2.   If it brings division, it is not a part of your destiny.
3.   If it has been destroyed, it is not a part of your deliverance.
4.   If it is not pure, it doesn't result in providence.

An unequally yoked, ungodly relationship is a part of what tears people down, but won't build them back up. Let it go and be free! The more we try to hold on, the more we miss the daily blessings God has planned for us. We can't focus on His plan, because we are so caught up in the past. The past is what it is, and we cannot change anything about it. The only thing we can do is build off the past to make better choices for the future. Avoid dwelling on what has happened and focus on a new plan—a God-spoken plan.

Anytime we choose to put something before God, we are giving it power. Have you given the power of God that lives in you over to such things as personal relationships, careers, money, selfishness, drugs, and alcohol? In Exodus 20:3 it states, "You shall have no other gods before me." Unfortunately we tend to put relationships before God and never give it a second thought. If you are in a relationship with a man and he is not your husband, having an intimate sexual relationship with him is not a characteristic God intended for us to have. We are

For God did not call us to be impure, but to live a holy life. Therefore, anyone who rejects this instruction does not reject a human being but God, the very God who gives you his Holy Spirit.

1 Thessalonians 4:7-8

rejecting God when we choose to disobey His Word. Allow doors to close to the wrong relationships in your life so God can open doors that will sweep you off your feet.

Sexual Relationships

A demon that some unmarried women wrestle against is fornication. We can make a conscious decision to not allow this demon to have authority in our lives. Being celibate is the ultimate choice when it comes to dealing with the sexual desires to keep our temples whole as daughters of the Most High. Why continue to give yourself to someone who is not a permanent part of your life and not your husband and who probably belongs to another woman? I choose to be celibate, because it is

For our struggle is not against flesh and blood, but against the rulers, against the authorities, against the powers of this dark world and against the spiritual forces of evil in the heavenly realms.

Ephesians 6:12

God's will and what He commanded. God is preparing me for a king who is deserving of every detail of my life.

I have heard people say, "I can't be celibate." Who are we that we can choose not to be celibate? There should never be a

My son (daughter), do not forget my teaching, but keep my commands in your heart, for they will prolong your life many years and bring you peace and prosperity.

Proverbs 3:1-2 (word added)

time when the words "I can't stop" are spoken. That puts flesh and man before God. HIV does not have a race, gender, or socioeconomic preference. Every time a woman has sex with someone who is not her spouse, her life is put at risk. A person may not show any signs and symptoms of being HIV positive and it is best for unmarried women to be celibate and married women to be loyal.

Having unprotected sex is like playing Russian roulette with your life, except the gun and bullet have been replaced with erotic behavior and sexual release. That one chance you take can change the course of your life, either with immediate death or a serious sexually transmitted infection. Do you really want to play Russian roulette with your temple, which was given by God? Don't pull that trigger; it may just be the final bullet.

Please don't be naïve and think it cannot happen to you. If you and your sex partner have the same thoughts, it is a dangerous combination and situation to put yourself in. Avoid anything that will heighten your sexual arousal and entice you to let down your guard and give in to sexual temptation.

Recognize prompters to temptation and make a conscious decision to prevent yourself from being in any proximity to that which will easily cause you to sin. Whatever temptation a woman is trying to be freed from (sex, drugs, alcohol,

No temptation has overtaken you except what is common to mankind. And God is faithful; he will not let you be tempted beyond what you can bear. But when you are tempted, he will also provide a way out so that you can endure it.

1 Corinthians 10:13

gambling) she needs to avoid going to the place where she is trying to break the chains of the habit. Don't go to the atmosphere that is choking the life out of you.

"But what if he leaves me after I tell him I'm celibate?" Bye! Let's be real: If he is a man of God seeking a relationship with you, it won't even be a choice on your part, because he will also bring celibacy into the relationship. If you are dating someone now and chose celibacy, let him know your thoughts and concerns for your relationship with God. "Oh, but he'll think I'm trying to trap him into marrying me." Not! Who do you serve: God or man? When everything seems to go wrong and life gets hectic, God will be the One who can save, heal, and deliver you. The man may decide to walk out, but "whoever gives heed to instruction prospers, and blessed is the one who trusts in the Lord" (Proverbs 16:20). Again I ask, "Who do you trust?"

One of the hardest things for us to do is forgive ourselves, particularly when it comes to fornication. I struggled with the inability to forgive myself for years. Have you ever had an instance where it was easier to forgive the person who offended you than it has been for you to forgive yourself? Not forgiving ourselves can cause us to miss doors that God has opened for us that were meant to propel us forward. How is this so? Satan will try to plant it in our spirit that we're not good enough to walk through the door because of past sins. But what does God say? Who do you trust?

Too many times, the problem may be that the woman has failed to realize that whatever situation she has found herself in that God is able to make a shift and remove her from the situation. Our heavenly Father is standing with open arms and ready to hold, comfort, and guide us into a place in our lives that is beyond measure. But the willingness to repent and change our thoughts and actions must be there.

God will reward those who take a stand and choose to live according to the instructions we have been given through

His Word. We must seek Him and His desires for our lives. Increase your faith and follow the instructions. Hebrews 11:6 states, "And without faith it is impossible to please God, because anyone who comes to Him must believe that He exists and that He rewards those who earnestly seek Him." Rewards come in other ways except financial, such as peace in your mind, heart, and soul. It can also include good health and genuine friendships.

Friendships

A friend loves you enough to tell you when you're wrong and not living right. A friend loves you enough to not support a wrong path you have chosen to take that is not in your best interest. It is a blessing to have true friendships, because those are the friends who will correct you and if you become offended can be easily mended by simply having a conversation with the person as if nothing ever happened.

A friend loves at all times, and a brother is born for a time of adversity.

Proverbs 17:17

A very close friend and I were going through life situations at the same time several years ago. Both of us realized that instead of confiding in and comforting each other, we dealt with it separately. This caused a strain in our relationship without either of us realizing what was going on. We may have been too proud to admit we were having issues or so caught up in what we were going through that we neglected the friendship and seemed to push each other away. While we felt the other should understand, this was not the case. Not communicating with each other was definitely the wrong thing for us to do. It caused an emotional strain within our relationship and caused us not to speak to each other for at least a year.

Since then, we have reached out to each other and had a great conversation with each other as if we never lost contact. This was the first step to mending the brokenness in our relationship. We have started spending holidays together and attending dinner party events together. I missed having her as a friend and her being a positive force in my life. Truly, I am grateful that God has allowed us to be restored: Broken No More.

On the other hand, some friends are meant to walk away, and it is predestined that they walk away at a certain point in your life. They may not be ready for the blessing God has in store for you, and He may want you to be able to have a firmer stand during your season. That may seem hard, but some of your friends are not ready to see the blessings and anointing that God has on your life. They are not ready for you to be moved to another level, and God has to level the field and only leave people in your life that can stand with you.

When the door appears to be closing on a friendship, just observe. Remain friendly, but observe. This way when the door closes completely, you are better prepared. Notice that I did not say totally prepared. None of us are totally prepared when a friend walks out of our lives without any reason or when we are instructed by God to remove ourselves from the friendship. When you know you have not done anything to cause discord in the relationship, but the other person started "acting funny" for no apparent reason, consider this: God knows that the person is going to be a hindrance and not a blessing to your life.

Then Naomi said to her two daughters-in-law, "Go back, each of you, to your mother's home. May the Lord show you kindness, as you have shown kindness to your dead husbands and to me. May the Lord grant that each of you will find rest in the home of another husband." Then she kissed them goodbye and they wept aloud and said to her, "We will go back with you to your people." But Naomi said, "Return home, my daughters. Why would you come with me? Am I going to have any more sons, who could become your husbands? Return home, my daughters; I am too old to have another husband. Even if I thought there was still hope for me—even if I had a husband tonight and then gave birth to sons— would you wait until they grew up? Would you remain unmarried for them? No, my daughters. It is more bitter for me than for you, because the Lord's hand has turned against me! " At this they wept aloud again. Then Orpah kissed her mother-in-law goodbye, but Ruth clung to her. "Look," said Naomi, "your sister-in-law is going back to her people and her gods. Go back with her." But Ruth replied, "Don't urge me to leave you or to turn back from you. Where you go I will go, and where you stay I will stay. Your people will be my people and your God my God. Where you die I will die, and there I will be buried. May the Lord deal with me, be it ever so severely, if even death separates you and me." When Naomi realized that Ruth was determined to go with her, she stopped urging her.

Ruth 1:8-13

Imagine if Ruth had decided to follow Orpah. She would have walked away from the very place where it was destined for her life to blossom with what God had in store for her. Ruth would have missed the opportunity to be a blessing and serve Naomi, her mother-in-law. Now that's a statement: serving our mother-in-laws. No matter whether we have a close bond or distant relationship with our mother-in-laws, they are still in the position of being our husband's mother.

Naomi felt that she didn't have anything else to offer Ruth and Orpah, and ultimately wanted them to go back to their own homelands. The death of the two men affected three women and changed the course of their lives. A definite detour to the lives they had planned. Accepting detours in our lives can have positive outcomes if we are willing to yield and not fight against the changes. Detours often keep us from going into a dangerous zone, can take us to a higher level, help us in an area in which we need growth, and cause us to depend more on God than our own abilities. Do you complain and give up when facing a detour? Do you trust God's Positioning System when there is a necessary change in direction to help you reach your destiny?

If you continue reading the story of Ruth, you'll find out that she made the right decision and was exactly where she needed to be which resulted in having Naomi to provide guidance to her. Naomi assisted in getting Ruth ready for Boaz in her appearance, approach, and actions. Through God, she coordinated the steps of the next realm of life that they would enjoy together in the palace. Would Ruth have known what to do once she was in the presence of Boaz without Naomi's instruction? Ruth did not have a resistant spirit and humbled herself to the instructions necessary to transition them from desperation to deliverance.

Have you wondered what would have been Ruth's fate if she had followed Orpah instead of Naomi? How many of us have missed a blessing going down the wrong path? We've all probably known someone who missed a blessing following someone else. They were influenced by another individual to walk away from a company or family because of another person's desire to leave. In the end, their friendship did not last and those who truly needed the blessing, the follower, were left alone at the end of the journey. Make sure the person you are following is taking you to the mountaintop and not into the depths of a valley. Before you decide to follow a leader, make sure that leader is worthy to be followed. Consider what beliefs and people you're following. Are they leading you to or away from your destiny? Are you following someone or in a relationship with someone and trying to please the other person while making yourself unhappy and stressed?

Being in a relationship takes work—a lot of work. For example, a woman will make sure she is well put together for a date. We go out of our way to get our hair done, manicures, pedicures, and make sure our clothes are cute. How much effort is the man making we are trying to please? Women will get dressed up for a date only for him to arrive in a t-shirt, shorts, and flip-flops. We put a tremendous amount of effort into all of our relationships and have remained at risk for not being appreciated, which can summon the negative feelings to erupt.

Regardless of the type of relationship, whether it was a family member, friends, intimate relationship, or with co-workers, we have all experienced hurt and rejection. When someone hurts you, don't retaliate, because God is well aware of the person's mischievous ways and their intent to cause you pain. Don't respond in an ungodly way to an ungodly person or situation. The individual meant to hurt, shame, belittle, and destroy you, but in God we can find healing, hope, safety, and strength.

When dealing with a disheartening issue, use it as a learning process and an opportunity for character-building moments. There is always an opportunity to get revenge, but at the same time there is an opportunity to go beyond the expected reaction and demonstrate who you are in Christ. Make every effort to increase in faith and learn something from the undesirable situation.

Abusive Relationships

On average, nearly 20 people per minute, more than 10 million women and men per year, are victims of physical violence by an intimate partner in the United States. One out of every three women and one out of every four men have experienced physical violence by an intimate partner within their lifetime (National Center for Injury Prevention and Control, 2010). Domestic violence has continuously increased over the years with the most recent attention focused on relationships with professional athletes. To bring awareness that domestic violence will not be tolerated in the National Football League, several players have been featured in the 'No More' Campaign by participating in an anti-domestic violence video.

A fool takes no pleasure in understanding, but only in expressing his opinion.

Proverbs 18:2 ESV

When a woman grows up witnessing domestic violence, she may naturally think that this is the expectation during a relationship. She may not have been exposed to a loving and gentle relationship as a child and believes that what she has witnessed is normal for any relationship. Unless she decides to break the cycle, she will find herself in the same type of relationship as an adult.

Having been in several abusive relationships, I speak from experience in knowing that it is hard for some women to break from the cycle of abuse. Although I witnessed love and adoration with my parents, I knew the abusive relationship I found myself in wasn't normal but didn't have the confidence and strength to walk away. Each time I left, I somehow found my way back into something that was not good for me. Some of my rationalizations for returning were: "It's my fault.

He apologized, said he changed and things will get better. I shouldn't have made him mad. I love him and he really does love me." It was a myriad of unrealistic excuses.

The most humiliating times in my life occurred in one of the relationships where I was thrown out of the apartment in my underwear and in another relationship begging not to be beaten while on a drive out to the field. When I was put out of the apartment, I did what was natural, ran for my life, and hid behind a bush until someone passed by and called a friend for help. I could not figure out why this was happening to me at 18-years-old. It is not natural to be in an abusive relationship, yet something had drawn me in, and it was hard to break away, even after such humiliating events. Two stabbings later, one to my right arm while shielding myself during one of our fights and several months later when he was stabbed by a girl I caught him with; I realized that I needed to be free from that relationship.

As if that wasn't enough, I found myself in another abusive relationship. In one incident, I had been in a parking lot fight with my boyfriend after ramming into his car because he was sitting a little too cozy with another female. Much of this event, I don't remember because he physically attacked me, and I was admitted to the hospital for overnight observation. Truthfully, I should have stayed at home that night instead of going to look for him. As with most young, college female students, the best judgment is not always practiced when we are caught up in a destructive relationship. "Know this, my beloved brothers: let every person be quick to hear, slow to speak, slow to anger; for the anger of man does not produce the righteousness of God" (James 1:19-20 ESV). I remember having to practice this scripture after returning from attending a college weekend Bible conference in Hot Springs, Arkansas in which this scripture was used in one of the teachings.

The scripture worked well for me because several days after the accident, my ex-boyfriend and I were having a conversation about fixing the car. He was yelling and cursing in the telephone and not trying to listen to anything I was saying. Each time he would call and yell at me, the response was, "When you calm down and want to talk, I will listen." I had every intention of paying for the damage caused because of my reckless actions. Eventually he calmed down and we were able to have a somewhat decent conversation to move toward getting his car repaired. The only thing I could remember as he was yelling in the telephone was to be slow to speak and slow to become angry as I dealt with my inner emotions and his outward and obvious anger. We have to have God's Word imbedded in our heart to deal with highly emotional conversations.

Whoever restrains his words has knowledge, and he who has a cool spirit is a man of understanding.

Proverbs 17:27

In another relationship, I repeatedly was taken out in a field and beaten with a whip like an animal. The whippings occurred at night and in the middle of an open field in the country. The whip was burgundy with a long cord and was like the ones seen in the western movies used to keep the cattle in line. It was a humiliating experience and one that left painful lashes on my body that have since healed. I was forced to get out of the car, take my shirt off, and be expected to take the whipping without rejection. I could not believe what was happening to me and could not understand how someone who claimed to love me could be so cruel. No one could hear my screams and cries for help. The pain from the lashes of the whip is indescribable and scarred me mentally and emotionally for a very long time. Although I knew what was happening was wrong, I was afraid to press charges and report him. I was in desperate need of counseling and guidance, but chose to stay silent.

If you are in an abusive relationship, seek help immediately. The National Coalition against Domestic Violence Hotline number is 1-800-799-7233. Many women remain in and return to abusive relationships out of fear. Women have also become the abuser in relationships. Just as with HIV, abuse does not have a socioeconomic status, religious, cultural, or ethnic preference. Take the steps needed for protection from future harm and possible death.

According to the Mayo Clinic in 2011, it might not be easy to identify domestic violence at first. While some relationships are clearly abusive from the outset, abuse often starts subtly and gets worse over time. You might be experiencing domestic violence if you're in a relationship with someone who:

- Calls you names, insults you, or puts you down
- Prevents you from going to work or school
- Stops you from seeing family members or friends
- Tries to control how you spend money, where you go, and what clothes you wear
- Acts jealous or possessive or constantly accuses you of

being unfaithful
- Gets angry when drinking alcohol or using drugs
- Threatens you with violence or a weapon
- Hits, kicks, shoves, slaps, chokes, or otherwise hurts you, your children, or your pets
- Forces you to have sex or engage in sexual acts against your will
- Blames you for his or her violent behavior or tells you that you deserve it
- Portrays the violence as mutual and consensual

Source: *(Mayo Clinic, 2011).*

It is important that we notice any character changes in our friends who may be involved in an abusive relationship. She may not openly express to anyone and admit that the abuse is occurring, but as her friend, you owe it to her to ask questions. I would encourage you to ask her in person instead of over the telephone. We know how to masquerade on the telephone, but in person, body language can make all the difference to what is actually said. Pay attention to her facial expressions, her eyes to see if she tears up, and her body language. Let's not turn our heads when we see or suspect domestic violence is occurring. According to the National Coalition against Domestic Violence:
- One in every four women will experience domestic violence in her lifetime.
- An estimated 1.3 million women are victims of physical assault by an intimate partner each year.
- 85 percent of domestic violence victims are women.
- Historically, women often were victimized by someone they knew.
- Females who are 20-24 years of age are at the greatest

risk of nonfatal intimate partner violence.
- Most cases of domestic violence are never reported to the police.
- Almost one-third of female homicide victims that are reported in police records are killed by an intimate partner.

While in the relationships, I was stabbed in the arm, had a broken nose, choked to near death, and had a hot iron placed against my left leg, which is now a permanent reminder of an abusive past. Sadly, I have lost a baby as a result of physical and emotional abuse. Throughout all of this, God kept me, spared my life, and removed me from the relationships.

Women who suffer from domestic violence will eventually suffer from a loss of self-worth, decreased self-esteem, and will find that she is broken and left with feelings of hopelessness. This will occur over an evolved time, and she may eventually find that her thoughts are focused on suicide. She may feel that God is silent in her life and that He has forgotten about her. God never forgets His daughters and wants them to have His peace, joy, love, and order in their lives. He is a God of order and not confusion. If you are in an abusive relationship or know someone who is, take immediate action to be removed from the situation to prevent further undue harm. Do not be afraid because God is with you. There is no hurt that God does not feel and that He cannot heal.

I married my second husband…twice. We were married November 2005, divorced October 2011, remarried April, 2012 and divorced again in December 2012. We sought Christian counseling on several occasions. Somehow he had come to the conclusion that it was within his right not to work, but to receive the blessings. His focus was solely on being the pastor of a church in which he was not receiving a salary. Taking care of one's own home will indicate whether a man has the ability to lead and rule over the things of God.

Remember I mentioned earlier in the book that I was working three jobs to meet our needs at home and help with the church finances. I was teaching at Carrington College, University of Phoenix, and working a night shift on the weekend at Good Samaritan Medical Center. There were times during the week that my workday started at

God has heard my prayer and has seen my tears; He is healing me.

2 Kings 20:5b

6am and did not end until 10pm. On Fridays, I was in the office from 7am to 5pm, went home for a quick sit-down and was at the hospital to work a 12-hour shift from 7:00pm to 7:30am. I needed a schedule to keep up with the schedule.

It was during this time that I started slipping into darkness. There was a feeling of being in a relationship, yet feeling alone, unappreciated, and unloved. After returning home from a 14-hour workday, I asked my ex-husband to go downstairs and warm up leftovers from the day before so that I could eat after taking a shower. His reply was "no." Standing at the foot of the bed, I felt anger, resentment, emptiness, and useless. It was as though there was nothing else to give. Second Thessalonians 3:10 says, "The one who is unwilling to work shall not eat."

I don't even know where to start with how this scripture was playing out in my home. Other than saying, my ex-husband spent at least three years not working, but ate plenty, traveled, and enjoyed the blessings of me working day and night. This began to place harmful wear and tear on me mentally, spiritually, emotionally, and physically.

I believe at that very moment, my inner being snapped, and I lost confidence in him, our marriage, and me. However, it had not snapped enough for me to actively do something about it. I was working tirelessly day in and day out, only to come home and not receive the care and comfort from the one person I should have been able to depend on. He was wearing the pants, but I was putting in the work. Entering into brokenness, I became unemotional into the reality of the marriage.

It became frustrating working the long hours only to come home to the same emptiness night after night. I became a sad person on the inside while maintaining an outward appearance that everything was OK. As a pastor's wife, we are unfortunately expected to be strong at all times. I was told by another pastor's wife that there was an expectation, unspoken or otherwise, that as a pastor's wife I was to uphold the home and accept that my husband was going to forget about me and take care of others first. I had enough sense to know that this was unacceptable.

No leadership position, career, hobby, or person should ever come before a marriage. In Colossians 3:18-19 it states, "Wives, submit yourselves to your husbands, as is fitting in the Lord. Husbands, love your wives and do not be harsh with them." Just as a wife is to submit, honor, and love her husband, the husband has the responsibility of providing for his wife, loving her, and honoring her with his substance. Husbands are given these instructions in Ephesians 5:25: "Husbands, love your wives, just as Christ loved the church and gave Himself up for her." It is never in the plan for a wife to do all and be all in a marriage. She needs her king to be a king.

I knew divorce was not what God intended for my marriage and could not understand why it had taken such a drastic turn from what our relationship was like in the beginning. There was a deep desire and longing for my marriage to work, but unfortunately, the shift to me being the only one bringing in income caused brokenness in me and in the marriage. In no way am I trying to imply that everything I did was right in the marriage. What I am saying is that I definitely tried to be the best wife I could be for him.

Knowing that my marriage was unsuccessful once again, I needed to get additional insight. We were having dinner at my home one Sunday after church, and I asked a friend's father the question "What happens when you know that God told you that someone is going to be your husband, and it did not work out?" In paraphrasing his answer, he said that somewhere in the relationship the chain was broken, and it got off path. God can reveal something to you, but if it gets off course from His plan, He may choose to release you and place you on a different path. Somehow we got derailed and weren't able to get back on track.

After trying everything I could and realizing that my heart was continuing to be void of positive feelings and love, I filed for divorce. I needed to be protected from self-destruction and needed to be free to breathe again. It was heartbreaking, but necessary and I realized that the longer I stayed in the marriage, the more broken I had become. I am not advocating divorce and encourage you to pray and listen for the Holy Spirit to be your guide. Abuse of any kind is not acceptable in a relationship and as a result God's blessing sometimes includes removing certain people, events, and plans out of our paths in order to hear from Him and go in the direction He is leading us.

As I've stated before it is a good idea to make scripture personal and speak the scripture over your life. There are going to be days when Satan is on serious attack to keep you in a depressed mood or in an unhealthy relationship. Satan

May the God of hope fill you with all joy and peace as you trust in him, so that you may overflow with hope by the power of the Holy Spirit.

Romans 15:13

will fight you throughout the day and along the journey to keep you from doing what is needed to have a better day and become a better person. He will put obstacles in your way and invade your thoughts with negativity. Refuse to entertain his negativity and any traps placed along the path. Just as Satan is relentless in persuading people not to trust God, we need to be relentless in praying and saying who we are in God and "praise Him because, we are fearfully and wonderfully made" (Psalm 139:14).

Fasting and praying will help us receive freedom, break the chains, move forward, and not go back to the way things used to be. "However, this kind does not go out except by prayer and fasting" (Matthew 17:21). By including fasting with our prayer life, we can break chains and be empowered to make necessary changes in our lives through the Holy Spirit speaking to us in the still quietness of His presence. If there is any area in your life that you need clarity, I encourage you to fast, be still and cut out the busy-ness to allow time to hear what the Holy Spirit is speaking to your heart.

Monica DeBro

Chapter Six:
Always in My Heart

He will not always accuse, nor will He harbor His anger forever;
He does not treat us as our sins deserve or repay us according to our
iniquities. For as high as the heavens are above the earth, so great is His
love for those who fear Him; as far as the east is from the west, so far
has He removed our transgressions from us.

Psalm 103:9-12

Having an incompetent cervix, trauma from an accident, still birth, physical and mental abuse and abortion are all factors that have caused women not to carry a baby to full-term delivery. Hopefully something discussed in the few pages of this chapter will help someone who needs to be healed and delivered from brokenness as a result of a baby that is always in your heart, but not in your arms. In some way each of us has been affected by the loss of a baby, either personally or with a relative or friend. On a personal level, I've had the unfortunate experience of having a miscarriage and an abortion. Neither was easy, but I thank God for His healing and forgiveness. Was the loss of the baby because of one or more of the following?

- Natural causes
- Stillbirth
- The result of a car accident or other trauma to the abdominal area
- Caused by drug or alcohol use
- The result of a miscarriage related to a domestic violence relationship, either verbal or physical
- A decision to have an abortion because of pressures from family, husbands, friends, and boyfriends
- A decision to have an abortion because the pregnancy was the result of a rape

Do not judge, or you too will be judged.
Matthew 7:1

God wants you to know that He has the power of healing and forgiveness. He loves us and does not want us to suffer.

Initially, the only information that was going to be included in this chapter was a prayer of healing, personal forgiveness, and forgiveness for those who may have caused the loss. However, anything hidden cannot be healed. My past sins are different from yours, but we've all sinned and fallen short of the glory of God (Romans 3:23). Being healed and forgiven by almighty God is what matters and is important to me, not the judgment of others. I want to encourage you that if you have suffered through the pain of a miscarriage or an abortion, do not focus on the opinions or judgments of people. Become transparent and seek with urgency the healing power of God for restoration, healing, and wholeness.

The loss of a baby can cause a woman to have many hurtful feelings, thoughts, and regrets. One thing to remember is that we should never take this pain and direct it as anger towards God. We cannot allow Satan to implant in the roots of our heart a resentful and hating spirit toward God or toward individuals who hurt us and caused the baby to be removed from our lives. In reality, this is an unfortunate truth; some people may turn their backs on God because of things that have transpired in their lives. Not acknowledging what happened, the shattered feeling of not having fulfillment and any sin that may have been involved with not carrying the baby to full-term delivery can cause tremendous negative results.

Take necessary steps toward healing by first acknowledging what happened. Then, as we discussed in the first half of this book, pray and seek forgiveness from God and for others. Refuse to turn your back on God and your family and friends. Be bold in your prayers to God to receive from Him what you so desperately need.

God has the power to heal and we must trust Him to heal our wounds and the intimate pain in our hearts that He already knows we are feeling. He won't just cover the wounds; He, Jehovah Rophi, will heal the wounds. Release your hearts and wounds to God and don't allow Satan to steal your joy and make you feel as though the sin was so great that it doesn't deserve forgiving and a healing touch.

For years I pushed down and ignored the miscarriage and abortion that I experienced until I realized that not acknowledging it was causing excessive negative behaviors. When we don't acknowledge what has hurt us, we are subconsciously holding on to it, which in turn can prevent us from having healthy and whole relationships. Healing comes when we confess what is causing the hurt and earnestly petition God to pull us from Satan's grasp of discouragement and openly allow God to infuse us with His love and healing.

He heals the brokenhearted and binds up their wounds.

Psalm 147:3

I clearly remember the day I had the abortion and all of the emotions that were involved. I ran out of the house and got in the car frustrated and tired of hearing the nagging in the house about what I should do. The two-hour drive seemed to go by fast, and I found myself on the upper level floor of the building in the office where the difficult procedure would be carried out.

The details of that day are still vivid. I remember what clothes I was wearing, the paper I signed my name on, the pill I took to "relax" me, and being told to undress from the waist down to allow someone who did not care about me or my future to literally suck the life out of me. As harsh as it may sound, that is exactly what happened.

After finishing at this office, I had to drive another two hours to a family event occurring in another state. Imagine having to press through laughing and smiling with family members to celebrate during a happy occasion right after having an abortion. I looked a mess and felt even worse. It was as if I was an imposter among my family, and the real Monica did not show up that day.

When I was coerced into having an abortion, I coped with it by having an affair. I needed my ex-husband's comfort during the month of November when the baby was due to be born. I didn't receive this comfort, and Satan was aware of my feelings of loneliness and placed an ungodly situation in my path the month the baby was due to be born. I was working in the emergency room and was walking from one room to the next when I heard a male voice saying, "I see you're wearing a wedding band." That should have been the moment I took a stand for what was right. Unfortunately, I didn't take a stand but instead took off running down a crooked path of personal destruction.

This path included marijuana use, alcohol, lies on top of lies to cover up the first set of lies, and an adulterous affair. Even after moving to Phoenix, I was so caught up in the relationship that I was flying to different states to meet up with him. Living in a world of my own, I thought it was fun being picked up in limousines from the airport, taken to expensive restaurants, and staying in lavish places. I was "caught up" and thought it was comforting the numbness. In a subconscious way, I felt I was getting back at my ex-husband for not accepting the pregnancy. For me, it was all about getting even, but little did I know the pain that was waiting for me once I tore my family apart. The affair ultimately ended the marriage, and I take full responsibility for my part and accept that I could have found a better way to deal with having an abortion. I knew better, but did not do better and am not proud of my vengeful actions, reactions, or moments. It has taken a significant amount of praying, fasting, and reading the Word and books on healing to forgive myself.

Not only was there a need to heal from the hurt of an abortion, but years later when I saw him with a woman who had children much younger than our child would have been, a new pain started developing. In my quiet time, I started thinking about the reason he gave me for us not having the baby: "We just weren't ready." Ultimately, I got mad all over again and had to ask for strength to overcome. Does the rationale that "we just weren't ready" still hold true? Was the timing off or was selfishness involved? Of course, I could have stood my ground and kept the pregnancy. The choices I've made have panged and scarred me emotionally, but I've learned to move on and have a productive well-balanced life. I repented for the abortion and affairs and have since refused to place myself in ungodly relationships.

Maybe you can relate to the pain of losing an unborn child or maybe you know of someone who has. Take a few moments and pray the following prayer for yourself or intercede for a loved one. Where there is a blank line insert the name of the person you're praying for.

Prayer

Father God, in the name of Jesus, I pray and ask that You will heal _____ heart from the loss of the baby. Heal the hurt that has been embedded and harbored deep in her heart, which has taken root and prevented her from moving forward.

Father, I ask that You release _____ from this bondage and pain and not allow any future decisions to be affected by the loss of the baby whether it was by natural causes or through human actions. Your Word says in Matthew 11:28-30, "Come to me, all you who are weary and burdened, and I will give you rest. Take my yoke upon you and learn from me, for I am gentle and humble in heart, and you will find rest for your souls. For my yoke is easy and my burden is light." Father, I am seeking rest in Your arms.

In Jesus' Name. Amen.

Monica DeBro

Chapter Seven:

God's Blessings

*For the LORD God is a sun and shield; the LORD
bestows favor and honor; no good thing does
he withhold from those whose walk is blameless.*

Psalm 84:1

Every day is a blessing from God and a day to receive
God's blessing. What you do with the day will make all the
difference. God wants to bless us, but we have to make sure
that we are prepared so that we do not miss the blessing. In
order to step into the next level of success, we have to prepare
ourselves. The dream or vision that God has placed into our
lives requires active work to make the vision become a reality.
If we are not prepared when it is time to receive a blessing, we
will forfeit what God intended to be ours.

People who don't make plans to succeed may not be afraid
to fail, but afraid to succeed. In other words, the thought of
actually having success scares some individuals. They question
their ability to succeed and make statements such as "I'm not
smart enough. I don't have what it takes. It's a stupid idea and

nobody will invest in it." Trusting in God to fulfill what He promised and having confidence that you have the talent and abilities to excel will change the dream and vision into reality. Perseverance, responsibility, dedication, organization, and continuously producing within a timely manner are involved with being successful.

Has God instructed you to do something and you put it on the shelf? Is it on the shelf because it's not big enough for you and you want something grand? Or is it on the shelf because you don't think it is something you can fulfill? In both instances, God wants to see if you're faithful in the little things and to trust Him in areas that you think are too difficult for you to accomplish.

There will be times when you may not feel like working toward the vision and goal, but ask God for strength. There have been numerous times that I felt like I was out of words for this book. However, whenever I've committed time to God and the writing, He would pour the words into my heart and spirit. Small steps are steps. As the old saying goes: "If we take one step, He'll take two." Show God the faith He is deserving of by trusting that He won't lead you to the wilderness.

The following is a simple example of preparation to receive a harvest. A farmer doesn't wait until it is time for the crop to produce to plant. He has to assess the soil and see if it is good ground to plant the type of seed he wants to grow. He needs to have the correct tools, know whether to use compost or fertilizer, know which plants need to be planted indoors before replanting outdoors, and when and where to plant the seeds. Does the crop need direct sunlight or need some shade to produce? How much and how often does the crop need to

Now finish the work, so that your eager willingness to do it may be matched by your completion of it, according to your means. For if the willingness is there, the gift is acceptable according to what one has, not according to what one does not have.

2 Corinthians 8:11-12

be watered? Most importantly, he needs to know when the seeds are ready for harvest. You see, he does not wait until it is harvesting time to plant. He succeeds because he prepared by studying, learning, and planting at the opportune time. Planting in the right season will increase the possibility of ensuring that we will receive the harvest that is specifically designed for us. So, how does this apply to us? Well, if you want a successful business, you have to plant accordingly and do the proper research for it to be successful.

Are you praying and seeking God's favor to bless you with a promotion or better career? What preparations are you currently taking to be ready for when the opportunity presents itself with an open position? What would you do if the position you've been longing for suddenly became available and you were not prepared to apply for the position? Some employers offer leadership courses or conferences throughout the year for their employees. Are you taking advantage of these opportunities?

Avoid wasting time; relentlessly move toward the goal that is set deep inside of you. Although we all need time to relax and recuperate, sometimes, there can be a little bit too much time spent in this area instead of using the time to live out our purpose. Think about your current actions and attitudes to see if there is anything that is stopping you from being productive. If you are slothful about doing the work needed in your current position, how do you expect God to bless you with a position that requires you to be more organized, have better time management skills, discipline, hard work, dedication, and determination? Do you arrive to work on time? Do you take extra time on breaks or use work time to peruse Facebook? Successful employers will observe an employee's productivity before considering promoting the person to another position. The reason I say successful employers is because there are business owners and managers who hire friends to do a job that he or she is not qualified for and the end result is an unsuccessful business outcome.

Because of hard work, commitment, and loyalty, I was promoted to the assistant nursing program director position in November 2014. When the discussion initially started about me applying for the position, I had the defeating questions that I mentioned earlier in the book of not being good or smart enough. I had to cast down those thoughts and realize that God makes me good enough and will supply the wisdom I need to be in the position.

His master replied, "Well done, good and faithful servant! You have been faithful with a few things; I will put you in charge of many things. Come and share your master's happiness!"

Matthew 25:23

How you handle your personal finances also has an effect on receiving God's blessings in your life. Consider the subject of tithing. If you are not faithful with paying tithes on your current salary, is it realistic to expect God to bless you with higher pay in a position that would increase your tithes? We have to be committed to paying our tithes on the finances we have so that we can be committed to continue to pay tithes when the increase comes. As your finances increase, your tithes will increase. During a sermon on tithes, the Capital One commercial came to my mind: "What's in your wallet?" My response was, "Hopefully not your tithes!" When we are faithful in paying the tithes with little, He will bless us with more.

God's Parental Blessings

After my first divorce, I moved to Memphis, Tennessee in July 2005 but could not find peace in my spirit, heart, or mind. It was an unsettling feeling that would not go away and a never-ending cycle of not knowing what was going on. I had a great government job at the Veteran's Affairs Hospital and a part-time job working in the mother-baby unit at another hospital. The process was also being completed on purchasing a home. I found a church I liked and thought everything was going to work out.

However, the more I tried to press my way through and live in Memphis, the more intense the feelings of anxiety increased and the initial thoughts of suicide started to plague my mind. After praying, God revealed that I had not prayed about the move from Arizona to Tennessee, but I had decided on my own to move across states to continue an ungodly affair. God's answer was simple: "Go back." Without hesitation, my family was notified and surprisingly supported the decision. My brother-in-law is totally awesome and agreed to drive my possessions back to Arizona once I was settled with somewhere to live.

My parents were very close to my sons, and it was heartbreaking when my family moved to Arizona the first time. Having reconnected with them, my mother wasn't going to live miles away anymore. My mother made the initial decision to move and my father agreed. They were ages 73 and 78, and my other family members didn't believe they were going to move until the U-Haul truck was being loaded with their furniture and belongings on the same truck that was already loaded with my furniture. Our father was still the pastor of three churches in Arkansas and was quite busy for a man his age. He retired and moved to sunny Arizona—a totally different population from the 15,000-person town in Helena, Arkansas.

In the back of my mind I was thinking that I would have to move back to Arkansas or Tennessee if they are not able to adjust. Phoenix is much larger and busier, and they were getting up in age. How were they going to navigate Phoenix? They're going to get lost and don't have a mobile phone. How will I ever find them? I was weighing my own instincts

"Children, obey your parents in the Lord, for this is right. Honor your father and mother—which is the first commandment with a promise so that it may go well with you and that you may enjoy long life on the earth."

Ephesians 6:1-3

and thoughts and not considering that they had great mental capacities and if need be, could learn how to use a mobile phone. More importantly, God instructed me to move back to Phoenix and would take care of all of us.

My mother came to Phoenix first while dad finished the work needed at the church to transition new pastors into position. Mom spent her time getting their apartment fixed up and didn't go anywhere without me. The very first Saturday after my dad came, they were not at home the entire day.

The phone calls and drive-by visits to see if the car was in its parking space was continuous throughout the day. I had to work that night at the hospital and as a result of not knowing where they were, I didn't get any rest throughout the day.

Finally, at 6pm as I was pulling into the gate in the apartment community, I see their car backing up into the parking space. As I get closer, dad is shaking his head and laughing. When he got out I asked him what he was laughing at. His response: "You! 'Cause I know you been looking for us all day." I did not think it was funny at all. They had been over in Tempe shopping and exploring. When I asked him how they didn't get lost he responded, "We just watch the airplanes take off and land to know which direction to go." I was shaking my head, because they lived close to the airport and figured out the general direction to drive based on the airplanes. The one good thing about Phoenix is that the streets go all the way through without name changes, which made it much easier for them to explore. They went to Scottsdale and Mesa in the few years that they were here than I have in the 13 years I've been living here.

Mom worked until she was about 76-years-old. She liked her suits, purses, hats, and shoes. Plus, whenever the girls (my sisters, nieces, and I) decided to go on a vacation, she wanted her extra spending money. We paid for the trip, but she always wanted her extra. I smile, because she always seemed to have a suitcase packed for spur of the moment trips.

Now, the airplane trick didn't work so well with dad one night. He dropped mom off at work one night and decided to drive to U-Haul Storage and pay on their bill. When he tried to drive home, a dust storm was occurring and he went the wrong way. According to dad, several times he stopped to ask for directions, people would tell him to turn at the Walgreens. Who knows how many Walgreens were between point A and point B. By the time he finally stopped and decided to have someone call me, he was at a Circle K in northern Phoenix Cave Creek area, which is in the opposite direction of where we lived.

I found him sitting in the car sleeping when a bald man with a long beard, wearing a black leather vest, jeans, and boots started walking towards me. My initial thought was please don't hurt me. However, this gentle, giant, biker-looking man stated, "Is that your dad? I got him some water and waited until you got here because those dudes over there didn't look safe." Breathing a sigh of relief for this guardian angel, I was reminded to not judge a book by the cover. I thanked the man for watching after dad and the store clerk for calling me.

The years that I had with my parents were precious, personal, fun, and educational. There were Saturdays when my mother would call at 8am telling me that they were ready for their shopping day, which started with a stop to McDonald's for breakfast. However, if I asked them to be ready for church at 9:30am, the response was "that's too early for us to get dressed." I would just shake my head and wait another time to ask and the answer was always the same. On several shopping days, I was in the car sleeping, because they could put meaning to the saying "shop till you drop." It was always interesting when they went into the grocery store, got separate shopping carts, and went their separate ways to shop. Needless to say, they often came out of the grocery store with two of the same items purchased.

I recall one occasion when we were out running errands

and had to make a stop at Walgreens. My mother was going in the store to get my father's Ensure and medicine. She came up to his side of the car (he always rode in the front seat) and asked him to give her the money for the items. He thought about it for a few seconds, released his seat belt and said, "That's OK. I'll get it myself." It was a known fact that my mother rarely gave dad his change back from money.

On a different day, I went over to my parent's apartment to visit and settled in the recliner to take a quick nap. Usually, they would sit on the couch and watch television. This day was different, because I heard them rustling around the house. Suddenly dad said, "What are you looking for Pearl?" Her response, "My wig and you need to put your shoes on." I opened one eye to see them now fully dressed and walking swiftly from one room to another. I closed my eyes again only to hear my mother say, "We're ready missy." The rest of that story is clear … out the door we went. My parents were go-getters who provided priceless wisdom and loaded me with laughs. Parents should be honored, treasured, and taken care of as needed. I could give you numerous parent stories of the days and evenings we spent together. However, this next story was pivotal.

In June 2010, I was nudged by the Holy Spirit to go by my parent's home on the way to work. Normally, I wouldn't stop by until in the evening on my way home. When I went into the house I kissed mom who was in the kitchen cooking dad's breakfast. She informed me that dad had just walked back to the bedroom. When I entered the room, dad was lying with only his back on the bed. His legs were hanging off the side of the bed and his arms were drawn up to his chest. He was unresponsive and was in dire need of medical attention. Being a nurse, I knew instantly that his blood sugar was low and asked my mother to bring me some sugar to put under his tongue. As we were waiting for the ambulance to arrive, I was taking every measure I could to increase his blood sugar. Normally, you would not put anything into someone's mouth who is unresponsive. However, in this situation, there wasn't another option.

The ambulance arrived at the house and paramedics treated dad by giving him glucose through an intravenous (IV) needle in his arm to raise his blood sugar. Eventually, dad was responsive. However, upon their assessment, they did not see the need to transport him to the hospital for treatment. I refused to accept their decision and drove my father to the hospital emergency room. His last blood sugar at the house was in the 200s. By the time we got him dressed and took the 10-minute drive to the hospital where he was immediately assessed, his blood sugar dropped to the low 50s. Imagine if I had not taken additional measures to seek further treatment. Always trust the wisdom God bestows upon you.

That emergency room visit turned into a hospital admission to the intensive care unit, and my father receiving multiple diagnoses regarding his health. One of the diagnoses was that he had prostate cancer, and the doctor's prognosis was that dad had six months to live. Initially, it seemed as though a light went out of my dad's eyes, but it soon returned and he responded to the doctor, "You worry about me dying; I'll keep living." Dad never slowed down until the last two weeks of his life.

In December 2011, they decided to move back to Arkansas,

and I was concerned about the move. Both my parents received excellent health care in Phoenix. They had become accustomed to being active and having a variety of places to go and their activity level would be restricted in Arkansas. No matter how much I protested, they were determined to move. It wasn't until much later that I found out that my mother had received a cancer diagnosis while living in Phoenix and never shared this information with me until much later. This explained her urgency to move back to Arkansas. Both of them wanted their final resting place in Arkansas, and my mom had to see that my brother was doing OK. My mom was a fierce and feisty woman who wanted what she wanted and nothing less.

My mother passed away September 1, 2012 on my sister's birthday. The comforting part of this for me, in addition to God's comfort, was that my sister had taken dad to the hospital that morning instead of waiting until the evening. My dad prayed and sang to my mother, and I believe this eased both of their spirits. My heart aches but is comforted at the same time because my dad knew it wouldn't be long before she transitioned from life to death. I cannot imagine what my father may have been feeling knowing that his one true love of 65 years would no longer be there to make more memories. They put true meaning to the declaration of "to have and to hold until death do you part."

The Monday after my mother's service, dad moved to Carsen, California with my middle sister. Yes, at 82-years-old, he moved again. He did not want to live in Arkansas and made that evident in the weeks prior to mom passing. The look in his eyes pleaded with us to bring him back to Arizona or California. There was no question of whether his request would be granted. When the hospice nurse in California asked him what he wanted to accomplish he told her: "I want to go to the zoo." He had no intention of slowing down and every weekend was doing something different, such as going to Knott's Berry Farm, the museum, the zoo, and anywhere else he wanted to go.

My sister is a vegetarian, and she took the time to take cooking lessons to learn how to cook meals for him. This often required a call to our aunt in St. Louis for cooking tips. Dad was spoiled, and he deserved to be spoiled. My siblings and I spoiled both of our parents and I am proud of my family for their diligence in providing care to our parents.

During that time, I took numerous trips to California to spend time with him and still have a message on my phone from him that he was excited about me coming to visit. My sister and I spent hours at his bedside caring for him. One night, while in the hospital, he preached throughout the night and called out each of his children and grandchildren's name in prayer. It was a humbling experience as I lay across my bed of chairs and enjoyed listening to him pray and preach throughout the night. The last time I looked at the clock it was 1:15am, and he was still praying and preaching. Several days prior to this, he was not alert and not responsive to any treatment measures ordered by the doctors. He was not talking, walking, or acknowledging anyone. To hear him open up and start preaching and praying was God's blessing.

The next day as I was returning to his hospital room from getting coffee, the nurse stopped me and said that they could hear someone singing and checked several rooms before realizing it was him singing. When I went into the room, he was awake making his requests known. I asked him if he had been singing to the nurses, and he responded, "Yes, I needed to make sure they knew I was in here." That's my daddy!

I had previously told my sister that I had a dream that my nephew, Solomon, was going to be alone with dad when he passed and if that was to occur, she needed to be prepared to comfort him. On November 7, 2012, my nephew refused to go to school, because he wanted to stay with his grandfather at the hospital. My sister went directly to the hospital after getting off

Praise be to the God and Father of our Lord Jesus Christ, the Father of compassion and the God of all comfort, who comforts us in all our troubles, so that we can comfort those in any trouble with the comfort we ourselves receive from God.

2 Corinthians 1:3-4 (NIV)

work. Upon entering the room, she kissed dad on the forehead (as we always did) and said, "Dad, I'm here." He didn't respond so she repeated herself and looked at him again just as he was taking his last breath. My father transitioned from life to death in a gracious and loving way. God held him to keep my nephew from being alone in the room once he transitioned. God's love will always prevail!

Within a short time, both of my parents were resting in the arms of God. It was a difficult time but one that God guided all of us through. I'm not saying that we don't have days where we long for our parents' laughter, stories, and hugs. There are numerous days that I wish I could lay in my mom's arms or remind my dad that my name is not Laura or Carla and run my fingers through his curly hair. To feel close to them, I simply put on one of their sweaters or baseball cap.

Even though I walk through the darkest valley, I will fear no evil, for you are with me; your rod and your staff, they comfort me.

Matthew 25:23

I include this short story of my parents with the hope that you'll know that I understand loss. I understand pain and trying to recover from being a broken vessel. More importantly I know that God carries us through times that may seem too hard for us to handle. Believing and trusting in Him when everything may look like it is falling apart will cause some people to wonder how you're still standing and trusting in God.

Do what you know to do: Stand in faith believing that God can handle any situation better than we can ever handle it.

At the same time that I was dealing with my parents' imminent death, there was the looming end of a second failed marriage that I mentioned in an earlier chapter. My divorce to my second husband was finalized December 2012. Three definitive changes in my life had occurred within a four-month period. Dealing with three inevitable losses in a short period would cause some people to question God. If I had allowed Satan to have his way, any of these events could have pulled me further into darkness and swallowed me up into the pits of self-destruction once again. I chose not to allow that to happen but to seek comfort from the Father because the strong arms of God are more powerful than the enemy's schemes.

Chapter Eight:
God Will Provide

I had meticulously planned an important trip to Daytona Beach, Florida for my youngest son's National High School Drill meet, or so I thought. My flight was set, and I had reserved a room to stay at the same hotel as the drill team in order to minimize my son's stress, because he is very protective.

I arrived at the airport for a 1am flight scheduled to leave on Friday, May 3. The kiosk was not accepting the reservation number and a message kept showing that it was too early to print a boarding pass. After several attempts, I finally spoke with the ticket agent who informed me that the reservation was booked for Saturday, May 4 at 1am. This was a definite let down, and I could only blame myself for not paying attention to the reservation agent during the process of scheduling the ticket. I normally book my own flight online but decided to use the travel pass system and receive a 20 percent discount since my oldest son worked for the airline. In the end, that discount cost me another full-priced fare, simply because, I did not pay close attention to detail or check the email confirmation.

Obviously, leaving Saturday morning was not going to work, because the drill meet was scheduled to start at 8am and would be close to being over if the arrival time was for late

Saturday afternoon. Plus, I had to factor in the time it would take to get from the airport to Ocean Center Convention Complex, which is where the drill meet would be held. The ticket agent said it would be expensive for me to change my flight. While she was recalculating the cost of the ticket, the only thing that kept coming to me was a scripture, "And my God will meet all your needs according to the riches of His glory in Christ Jesus" (Philippians 4:19). I remained positive and refused to allow Satan to make me upset because of an error. The only thing I was concerned about was the amount of time it was taking the two ticket agents to complete the transaction. One agent would start then hand it off to another agent instead of completing the process. I knew I needed to get through security and at a major metropolitan airport that can be a process with the long lines. No matter the cost, I had to make this flight.

And I did. When I woke up at 5:45am on the flight, I thought on the experience and continued to think of Philippians 4:19. Even though I had to pay extra and had not planned on having to pay an additional cost for the airline ticket, God reminded me that all my needs were met. The mortgage had already been paid for the month and the car note was taken care of and paid ahead of schedule. God reminded me of the monies to come when I returned to Phoenix. And of course, He reminded me to pay more attention if I ever needed to make reservations by phone again.

Has there ever been a time when you realized a minor or major error was made and you allowed it to disturb your thoughts and cause a negative reaction? For every negative reaction, there is a consequence and missed opportunity to be strengthened and grow. There may be times when God will allow His children the opportunity to demonstrate faithfulness in Him through situations that will allow us to be more dependent on Him and grow as His daughters. For example, if there is a need for you to have more patience with people or situations, do not be surprised if there are continuous opportunities that occur in which you will have to practice patience.

Do not conform to the pattern of this world, but be transformed by the renewing of your mind. Then you will be able to test and approve what God's will is--his good, pleasing and perfect will.

Romans 12:2

It's unfortunate when someone has unrealistic expectations of asking God to make a change in them while expecting it to be done without some level of testing and pressure in order for the transformation to take place. As you are tested, thinking before reacting is always best to allow you to reflect on the situation before responding emotionally which can sometimes cause us to react the exact way in opposition of how we are seeking to change. Take advantage of opportunities that allow

God to transform you into to the person He desires for you to be. Before long, the character you want to present before God and man will be evident. Become triumphant in the test!

A Vessel Ready to Receive

In today's society, we have to be distinguished, because our light is deliberately designed to shine in a dark world. By having a different spirit, it will not be hard for the world to distinguish believers from unbelievers. The Bible states that Caleb had a different spirit than the other Israelites wandering around in the wilderness. He dared to believe God and His Word. In the midst of continuous complaining and negativity, Caleb had to renew his mind daily in order to not lose faith in God when he had to wait 45 years before seeing the Promise Land. He was leading a group of people who did not have faith and as a result had to suffer the consequences of their unbelief and unfaithfulness.

Caleb was 40 years old and God said the people would wander in the wilderness for 10 more years and that the generation that was 20-years-old and above would each die and not enter (Numbers 14:32-34). Imagine how Caleb must have felt knowing that he had to wait because other people did not believe. Nonetheless, Caleb did not give up. He remained faithful to what God had promised. Caleb kept his spirit ready to receive God's blessing no matter how long it took for the blessing to manifest.

Not trusting in God can cause a serious delay in the blessings to overflow. We live in a generation of urgency and wanting needs met instantly. Some people give up after 40

minutes if the need is not met. Forget having to wait 40
hours, 40 weeks, 40 months, or 40 years. I know what you're
thinking: "Lord, please don't let me wait 40 years." What
are you holding on to that could cause you to have to wait
longer for the blessing that God has revealed to you? Is it a
relationship? Is it a job or career? Are you afraid to step out
to make your dreams a reality? If it is something that God
has revealed to you and has laid out the path for you to take,
what are you waiting for? You have to move when the season
presents itself.

Blessings from Prayer

Although I was raised in the church, praying in tongues
was not a subject that was taught in the Baptist denominations.
I have become a part of a church family that acknowledges
the Lordship and Personhood of the Holy Spirit and exhorts
its members to receive the baptism of the Holy Spirit with the
evidence of speaking in tongues. Prior to receiving this gift, I
spoke with one of the church staff ministers after a midweek
service and told him I had not received the gift of the baptism
of the Holy Spirit. He could sense my hesitancy about praying
openly in the Holy Spirit. Each time we had a worship service,
we would meet at the front of the church. He would pray, and
I would hesitate. After about a week of me praying, fasting,
and spending quiet time with God by not watching television
and having outside interferences, the minister instructed me
to stop fasting, go home, and allow God to bless me. He said,
"Tonight, you will receive the gift of the Holy Spirit."

I prepared for bed and was disappointed, because I did not

receive the gift and thought something was wrong with me. About 2am, I woke up and realized that my body was shaking and I was praying in the Holy Spirit. God saw the desperation that was intertwined in my spirit to receive His loving gift, and He provided it in His own timing. From my experiences, He likes to surprise me with an awe-inspiring delivery of blessings.

When we pray in the Holy Spirit, we must be careful not to make our own interpretations of what is being prayed. God will prepare our hearts to hear from Him when the time comes for the prayer to be revealed. There have been times when I prayed about something in the Spirit and God revealed it to me in subtle ways. It is as though He is speaking to my mind, heart and spirit all at once which results in a flood of emotions permeating through me.

When God reveals something to you, trust in Him that it will be fulfilled. Once He speaks to us, being in the holding phase and waiting on it to become a reality is not easy at times. Thoughts start to generate in our minds, such as, "OK, Lord, You showed this to me, what is the next step? How long do I have to wait before you make this come to reality?" Be patient. God is working it out on your behalf and will not let you down.

Take precautions about telling others what God has spoken to your heart. We must use protective measures to ensure that individuals do not derail our visions, dreams, and goals. There are some things that we need to keep to ourselves to keep others from interjecting and trying to make things happen. Waiting on God without telling anyone is not easy, because we want to share our excitement. However, if we pray about it and wait, once it does become reality, we will know that it was all God and not the help of others. Of course, this is going to depend on what God spoke to your heart and spirit. If it is something relating to your business, you may need to take necessary steps to make it a reality. Other times we may not need to make a move. God kept speaking to me, "Be still and know that I am God" (Psalm 46:10). We have to be patient and know that He has our best interest at heart. We are believers and must trust that God will supply all of our needs.

Going back to the story at the beginning of this chapter, as my thoughts became clearer after waking up at 5:45am on the flight, I realized a different need that was taking priority at that time, and I became frustrated. Not at the person who made the reservation and didn't understand my request. Not at myself for not paying closer attention to the travel dates. Not at the fact that I had to pay extra money for the ticket. I became frustrated because I was thirsty and didn't want to push the button and disturb the flight attendant for a glass of juice that was well paid for with my total ticket purchase. Laughter is healthy, so you have permission to laugh at this moment. This is how I felt regarding "disturbing" the flight attendant for serving me as a customer, which is a responsibility she carries in her daily work activities. It doesn't bother God for us to make requests to Him. In fact he instructs us to come to Him. He tells us to ask and said that He will supply all of our needs. God's riches are much greater than ours and because He is willing to give, we should ask, trust Him and have faith that He will provide.

Monica DeBro

Chapter Nine:

Moving Forward

And I pray that you, being rooted and established in love, may have power, together with all the Lord's holy people, to grasp how wide and long and high and deep is the love of Christ, and to know this love that surpasses knowledge—that you may be filled to the measure of all the fullness of God.

Ephesians 3:17b-19

God loves us beyond measure. No matter what we've done in the past, God's love continues to envelop our past so that it is not remembered, and He develops our future to fulfill His purpose. Our past is the past, and there is nothing that can be done to change it. No matter how much there is a desire to change what has happened in the past, it still remains unchanged. The blessing for us is that God does not remember our sins.

Although God does not remember our sins, it does not give us free will to sin. Our perfect God is well aware that disobedience to His Word will happen because of natural desires, impulsivity, irrational thinking, poor judgments, immediate desires, and the list can go on and on. "We all have sinned and fall short of the glory of God" (Romans 3:23). However, when we sin conviction will cause a true repentance in our actions, which will cause us to pursue God for forgiveness and not commit the sin anymore. Conviction is not meant to be comfortable. Conviction and comfort cannot occupy the same space. One of them has to go just as darkness must vacate when light arrives.

When we are convicted for something that we've done, it makes us uncomfortable. True repentance will require us to remove ourselves from relationships with certain people, employment, ungodly language, actions, and behaviors. It's impossible to continue to live in sin after being convicted of actions that are directly against the Word of God.

Repentance indicates a feeling of deep sorrow for what has been done and an increased understanding of who God is. It is unto Him that we sin: "Against You, You only, have I sinned and done what is evil in Your sight" (Psalm 51:4). As we go

I, even I, am He who blots out your transgressions, for My own sake, and remembers your sins no more.

Isaiah 43:25

from day-to-day and the pressures of the world are on us, we must remember that sins are against our Heavenly Father. The world may make sin seem like fun, but if your conscience is not clear, consider the source of the information that says "It's fun. It's a way of life. No one will see you." God sees everything and remember that the gift of repentance is from God.

Just as God remembers our sins no more, we are reminded to take into account Ephesians 4:32: "Be kind and compassionate to one another, forgiving each other, just as in Christ God forgave you." When someone causes us pain and later asks for forgiveness, we are to forgive them without requiring the person to grovel, beg, and plead. Here is the key that is often forgotten: We are to forgive each other just as Christ God forgave us. We cannot keep reminding the person of their sin and bringing it up whenever a disagreement occurs. This will only make the situation worse. The goal when a past sin is brought up is to make the person feel bad. This only causes the pain to grow deeper and the wound not to heal.

Removing the Bandages

True conviction and repentance will be the defining factor of whether an individual will continue to live in sin or turn away from sin. The person may have crying episodes and repeatedly say "Lord forgive me" with no true intentions to change his or her life. We often say "God knows my heart" and I encourage you to think about that. God does know our hearts and therefore knows if we are truly repentant or just trying to cover the sin with a bandage long enough for our feelings to be healed before committing the sin again.

Too many times, we try to cover a deep-rooted pain with a bandage when what we need is a debridement that will allow us to heal from the inside out. Debridement is used to clean dead and contaminated material from a wound to aid in healing. The procedure can be done to remove contaminated tissue, dead cells, decrease scarring and to aid in healing very severe injuries (NYU Langone Medical Center, 2013). With debridement, healthcare professionals get down to the root of the wound to start the healing process. With these types of wounds, if the doctor or nurse decided to simply apply a bandage to the wound, the person would never heal. The wound would be at increased risk of infection, which in turn would cause additional problems and possible loss of the limb or infection of other internal organs. How many internal wounds, emotions, and hurt feelings have you covered with a bandage that needs the attention of a deep cleansing and healing process that only God can provide?

There may have been times when we were forced to hide the wounds, but God has said that enough is enough. The time is now for you to receive healing over those hurts and

For I will forgive their wickedness and will remember their sins no more.

Hebrews 8:12

pains that have scarred you emotionally for years. Bandages are ineffective at covering the wounds such as molestation, rape, abortion, fornication, lying, stealing, adultery, unhealthy relationships, death of a loved one, and alcohol and drug use. It's time to remove the bandage and start the necessary healing by debriding the wound.

Throughout debriding, pain and delayed healing may occur. Pain because we have to go through the feelings of what caused the initial hurt and because it is sometimes difficult to forgive those who have maliciously hurt us. Pain because we have internalized what we did not want others to know and feel ashamed to bring it to the surface. Pain because we tell ourselves, "What if they don't believe me?" The delayed healing may occur as a result of being resistant to the leading of the Holy Spirit. "But when He, the Spirit of truth, comes, He will guide you into all the truth. He will not speak on His own; He will speak only what He hears, and He will tell you what is yet to come" (John 16:13). Are you willing to be led by the Holy Spirit to receive healing? Following the Holy Spirit may mean initiating contact with the person who hurt, denied, left, and betrayed you. It will mean forgiving the one person you trusted to protect you but only led you down a path of personal destruction for years. Are you willing to go through the pain of debridement to get rid of what has been infecting your heart, spirit, actions, and emotions for years?

It is time to stop allowing pain to have control over whom you are designed and wired to be. We are God's daughters, and He only wants the best for us and in order to receive His best, we have to "strip off every weight that slows us down, especially the sin that so easily trips us up. And let us run with endurance the race God has set before us" (Hebrews 12:1 NLT). The weight of the past and sin is slowing you down from running the race God has purposed for you and this is the season to strip it off and take off running.

Then He adds: "Their sins and lawless acts I will remember no more."

Hebrews 10:17

Although I am aware that contents in this book may cause uneasiness for others, it is a weight that I am stripping off because I followed the leading of the Holy Spirit to allow Him to debride my wounds and remove the necrotic dead tissue that was preventing me from healing. My prayer is that it will allow others to be transparent and open up a door of healing. We hide behind too many things because we don't want anyone to know. These are weights that slow us down and God wants us to be free to run the race that He established for us.

Monica DeBro

Closing Thoughts

Now unto Him that is able to keep you from falling, and to present you faultless before the presence of His glory with exceeding joy, to the only wise God our Savior, be glory and majesty, dominion and power, both now and ever. Amen.

Jude 1:24-25 (KJV)

We can't blame another man or woman for the decisions we've made and actions we've taken. Even if someone seeks the help of a pastor, counselor, financial advisor, or life coach, the final decision rests in the hands of each individual of what he or she will ultimately do with the information provided. The personal decisions that we make without seeking God can have devastating results in our lives, and we must be willing to accept the outcome. These decisions include, but are not limited to, acting on something that God specifically and directly told you not to do as well as not doing something that God instructed you to do. Are you doing what God told you to do or are you passively waiting for it to be fulfilled?

Has God instructed you to do something and you're still sitting around waiting on the sound of the trumpet before taking action? Don't let the sound of the trumpet that you are waiting to hear be the one described in 1 Corinthians 15:52. I encourage you to be diligent in what God has purposed in your heart because you never know whose life will be impacted by your obedience to God.

While going after what God has placed in your heart, avoid giving up your time to people and events that are not of God or a part of your destiny. If you don't have a vision, pray to God and seek His help to know and understand the vision for your life. In Habakkuk 2:2, the Lord instructs us to write down the vision that is revealed to us. It is important to write down the vision and keep it in front of you so that when life happens, you won't easily forget what you have been instructed to do. Let's be honest: We don't always act immediately and consistently on what God tells us to do. Written reminders and nudging from the Holy Spirit can boost us into action to get on and stay on course to see dreams and visions fulfilled. What steps do you need to take to fulfill your destiny?

Earlier in the book, I discussed the need to surround yourself with praise and worship music in order to make it through the seasons of healing and to help you remain focused on God. This is a list of songs that have helped me to make it through each day and each stage of debridement. Avoid waiting until you're in the midst of darkness to start studying God's Word and listening to praise and worship music. Hide His word in your heart so that when the attacks of Satan come, you can overcome it with the scriptures and songs dwelling on the inside of you.

- "Free"–Kierra Sheard
- "Take Me to the King"–Tamela Mann
- "I Won't Go Back"–William McDowell
- "Our God is Awesome"–Charles Jenkins

- "Moving Forward"–Israel Houghton
- "I'm Not Ashamed"– Ricardo Sanchez
- "Lord Make Me Over"–Tonex
- "Nobody Greater"–VaShawn Mitchell
- "Change"–Tremaine Hawkins
- "Break Every Chain"–Tasha Cobbs
- "If I Can't Say a Word"–Ann Nesby
- "Restoring The Years"–Donald Lawrence

God places people in our lives to help us when we are struggling or in a place of darkness. He is always available to help us throughout the healing process and yet also understands our need of comfort from each other. As women, we have to be willing to open ourselves up and acknowledge that we are struggling in an area that is trying to take us out of the will of God. Unfortunately, we have the tendency to allow pride, shame, guilt, thoughts of being judged, and sometimes resistance to keep us from opening up to receive the help and healing we desperately need and long after. Make a conscious decision and take action toward lifestyle changes that will ultimately propel you to the original designed destination.

It is never too late to make decisions that will change your destination and put you on the right path. Think about the crucifixion and the response of one of the men on the cross next to Jesus and the decision that was made in the final hours of his life. "One of the criminals who were hanged there was hurling abuse at Him, saying, 'Are You not the Christ? Save Yourself and us!' But the other answered, and rebuking him said, 'Do you not even fear God, since you are under the same sentence of condemnation? And we indeed are suffering justly, for we are receiving what we deserve for our deeds; but this man has done nothing wrong.' And he was saying, 'Jesus, remember me when You come in Your kingdom' And Jesus said to him, 'Truly I say to you, today you shall be with Me in Paradise'" (Luke 23:39-43 New American Standard Bible). He did not have a defeated, woe-is-me, and I've-done-wrong-and-am-condemned-to-Hell attitude. He did not give up but made it up in his mind to go after the opportunity to live eternally with the Savior. His desire was to have a greater ending than the life for which he was being punished and did not think it was too late to be saved. In the final decision, there was an instant change in his destination because of the acknowledgement and accepting of Jesus as Lord and King.

Jesus answered, "I am the way and the truth and the life. No one comes to the Father except through me."

John 14:6

Consider this: The man knew who Jesus was before he got to the cross, but continued to live the lifestyle which caused him to lose his earthly life at the same time Jesus was being crucified. Imagine if he had not gotten caught and subjected to punishment at that appointed time? Since he knew who Jesus was, he had the chance to accept him before the day on the cross and had the chance to make better decisions. Ultimately, being on the cross next to Jesus saved his eternal destination. Do you know who God is, but choose to hold back on accepting Him as Lord and Savior? If so, pray this prayer:

Prayer

Heavenly Father, I come to you in the name of Jesus and repent of my sins. I believe that Your Son, Jesus Christ died and was raised from the dead with all power of Heaven and Earth in His hands. His blood has cleansed me from sin and because He suffered, I am free from condemnation. Please forgive me of my sins, known and unknown, and help me to turn away from sin. Thank You for loving me enough that while I was a sinner, Christ died for me. I invite You to come into my heart and life today. Change me and make me a vessel for You.

In Jesus' Name, Amen.

We have all at some point in our lives been broken or had broken hearts. As believers in Christ, we should know that God is always with us, even when we feel broken. He is the Potter who can mend brokenness, who can put us back together and make us into a better vessel than we were before we became the lump of clay broken and unrecognizable to ourselves, family, and friends. Whether the brokenness occurred as a result of a negative impact from relationships, jobs, children, finances, abuse (whether self-inflicted or caused), something caused you to be broken and God is ready to start debriding your wound and bring complete healing and restoration.

Praying is essential to putting the broken pieces back together. Thank God for intercessory prayers and prayer warriors. "In the same way, the Spirit helps us in our weakness. We do not know what we ought to pray for, but the Spirit himself intercedes for us through wordless groans. And he who searches our hearts knows the mind of the Spirit, because the Spirit intercedes for God's people in accordance with the will of God. And we know that in all things God works for the good of those who love him, who have been called according to his purpose" (Romans 8:26-28). God's desire is for us to believe in Him and trust that He is who He says He is and will fulfill what He has promised. It wasn't meant for you to be broken, arise and allow the Potter to restore you.

But now, O Lord, you are our Father; we are the clay, and you are the potter; we are all the work of your hand.

Isaiah 64:8 ESV

REFERENCES

Center for Disease Control and Prevention: National Center for Injury Prevention and Control (2010). Accidents or Unintentional Injuries
http://www.cdc.gov

Elisabeth Kübler-Ross Foundation: Five Stages of the Grief Process and quotes by Elisabeth Kübler-Ross (1926-2004) http://www.ekrfoundation.org/

Mayo Clinic (2011). Domestic violence against women: Recognize patterns, seek help. http://www.mayoclinic.com/health/domestic-violence/WO00044

National Coalition Against Domestic Violence http://www.ncadv.org/files/Dome sticViolenceFactSheet(Nationa l).pdf

NYU Langone Medical Center (2013, December). Debridement of Wound, Infection, or Burn. http://www.med.nyu.edu/content?ChunkIID=14803

U.S. Department of Health and Human Services (n.d.). Human Immunodeficiency Virus (HIV) Fact Sheet. http://www.hhs.gov/opa/reproductive-health/stis/hiv/

Young, S. (2012, November 9). CNN Health, Imprisoned over HIV: One man's story. http://www.cnn.com/2012/08/02/health/criminalizing-hiv/index.html

Monica DeBro

Made in the USA
San Bernardino, CA
01 May 2015